360° Feedback

A Transformational Approach

Elva R Ainsworth

360° Feedback

First published in 2016 by

Panoma Press Ltd
48 St Vincent Drive, St Albans, Herts, AL1 5SJ, UK
info@panomapress.com
www.panomapress.com

Book design and layout by Neil Coe.

Printed on acid-free paper from managed forests.

ISBN 978-1-784520-70-0

DEDICATION

This book is dedicated to my mother, Dr Marion S Ainsworth, who passed away exactly a year before writing started – always interested and for ever enquiring, she inspired us all.

CLIENT FEEDBACK

"I think your insight and deeper dives into the application of 360 and your learnings are hugely useful."

"The external consultant should also have this as a must-read."

Helen Hunter, Head of Talent Development, Heathrow

"Elva's rich and extensive experience is the best possible guide through the 360 minefield."

Colin Coombs, Learning and Development Consultant, Tate

"This is just the sort of resource that is missing for HR practitioners.

Very few books take you through the detailed process to operate a 360 degree, so this is very useful and accessible."

Anna Petts, Head of OD & Learning,
University of the Arts London

"It demonstrates what a powerful transformational tool 360 can be."

"This is a fantastic, practical and inspiring book, which I think should add a lot to the successful implementation of transformational 360 processes in organisations."

Liz Bridge, Learning Services Director,
Centre for Customised Executive Development,
Cranfield School of Management

"It's a great book and gives a fresh perspective."

"Twenty years of experience is evident in every word on the page. What company wouldn't want that insight! Insights into discovering the data you have and will gain, and ways to interpret it. This book dares you to be innovative with how you use and present that data."

Mark MacKenzie MBE, Organisational Development Advisor,
Transport for London

ACKNOWLEDGMENTS

Thank you first to my dedicated team at Talent Innovations who tirelessly encourage and support my work in this area. Specifically to Karen Smith, Alicen Stenner and Stephanie Warnes who have waited patiently for this book to be written; to research assistant Dr Rafia Faiz and graphic designer Greg Tansey who with Tim Sawers and Jo Ainsworth provided all the graphics.

Special thanks to my brother Mark who agreed to code my first 360 degree feedback instrument way back in 2000 while recovering from a skiing accident, and later joined me to build a serious and successful player in the market.

Finally, thank you to all our clients over the last 20 years who have given me and my team permission to design and deliver 360 projects. It is a total privilege to work with people on their personal 360 degree feedback data and one I do not take lightly.

Thank you.

CONTENTS

INTRODUCTION

This is all about 360 degree feedback[1] but it is not *just* about 360. This book is written as a thorough and practical review of all the critical factors you need to consider when you are introducing 360 degree feedback into an organisation. It covers how to position it, how to design the instrument and the report, how to deliver 360 data so it works and how to unpick the emotional reactions you may get from it. From over ten thousand hours of hands-on experience, it gives you examples of how 360 degree feedback can be done and how it can be done just right for your environment. Overall, it describes an approach designed and tested to have a truly transformational impact.

In order to do this it covers how best to approach your role as a change agent[2] in HR (or as a consultant or coach) and ultimately how to change people. This thinking has emerged from a commitment to deliver 360 degree feedback as an effective developmental intervention but naturally also applies to other types of intervention, so you may discover a broader application of the key ideas and concepts. They have been discovered through dedicated experience of almost 30 years of operating in what is a deeply resistant culture here in the UK. A taste of the USA, which has a more self-expressive environment, demonstrated how resistance itself was significant which then led to a journey of discovery to work out how on earth HR can truly influence in these conditions. Hopefully you will see that it is possible to make a difference. It may take huge ingenuity and creativity along with a big dose of determination but it is worth it.

There is a whole new way for work to be – one where everyone is fully satisfied; where talents are tenderly nurtured and growth is extraordinary; where there is a clarity of purpose and a strong sense of fulfilment; where results are co-created and the organisation is fully integrated into the community. HR has a special place in this future in that, if this were true, HR would be redundant yet at the same time could be wonderfully proud of being at the source of this new way. Hopefully you will see how a well-designed and carefully executed 360 degree feedback survey can help you get there.

CHAPTER 1

It's not your job to change your managers

"All you can change is yourself, but sometimes that changes everything!"

Gary W. Goldstein
(Producer of Pretty Woman)

"It was 1992. I was heading up the corporate HR function at the RAC Motoring Services and I was exasperated! Our newish intern was driving us crazy. He was bright and desperately keen to learn but way too eager to help. All my team were complaining as he kept getting in the way. I had tried all our usual tactics – asking him to stop, personality profiling, others giving him feedback, even getting irritated with him, but nothing worked. I had heard of this new thing called '360 degree feedback' so I tried this (it was an early form, based on a personality profile). Surely we in HR are supposed to be able to change people's behaviours?

"Everyone was delighted to be able to give him full and detailed feedback. He was happy to have some attention and I simply showed him the results. It was clear – he saw himself as very caring, supportive and sensitive to feedback and literally everyone else saw him as quite the opposite on these traits. He took it in and went quiet. I acknowledged that I thought this reflected his clear intention to support us all and thanked him for this. I waited and finally he looked up at me and apologised profusely: 'I will stop trying so hard and start listening'.

"He was a terrific team member from that moment and I was hooked on 360."

This was the start of my journey into 360 degree feedback. It was a glimpse of the potential power of this magical intervention. In the years since then I have discovered tricks and methods to guarantee this magic and this book is written from a passionate desire to share what I have learnt with anyone wanting to cause transformational shifts in their working relationships and in their organisations. There are tips and examples in every chapter. There is full information and guidance on how to design a 360 degree feedback survey for success, how to interpret a report and how to run a project with ease as well as how to ensure someone leaves upsetting data feeling OK. People matter, so if you believe this, hopefully there will be something for you in this book.

Because *"business is about people"*[3], and people matter, it seems logical to conclude that effective human resources is crucial. Good people strategies and processes are critical for good business. You know this. You see examples of this all the time. You see when the people processes work well and when they do not. You see how this leaves employees and you see how the worst can behave and how the best can leave! You can end up with good employee engagement, healthy innovation and a highly motivated workforce, or alternatively you can get grievances, performance issues, unresolved conflicts, disappointing results and dysfunctional team-working. Or all of the above.

You can see the link between people processes and these results. This is the area you can impact and it is also your job to manage some of these processes, so naturally you work hard to improve them. But they are not your processes. The fact is that the people get managed by the business, not by the HR function. They get fired by the line, they get appointed by the line. They get promoted and demoted by the line. They get appraised by the business, they get leadership from the business and they get rewarded by the business. HR can advise, facilitate and guide and can try to direct the line but ultimately the accountability is with the line. This is the conundrum of HR.

According to the Chartered Institute of Personnel and Development (CIPD) your job is to *"champion better work and working lives by improving practices in people and organisations"*[4]. My view is that you, just as I was when I took my first HR job in 1985, have been set up to do an impossible job. The job of "improving the people practices" implies your job is to improve the way your leaders manage the organisation which implies there is something wrong with how they are right now. This deficit position is actually not a helpful starting point.

Let's just imagine for a while that someone was appointed from outside your family with the job to *"improve the communications"* in your family. The appointment was made by the head of the family (wonder who that would be?) and this person answers to them. How do you feel? Bit put out I should imagine. It immediately takes you to a position of defence and justification. You might wonder: *"What's wrong with my communications?"* *"What about him/her?"* or at least *"What's this about?"* You might even react with a *"No way are they going to change the way I communicate!"* There is something automatic that occurs when you know someone intends to change you. This is what you in HR are dealing with all the time – let's call it resistance.

Despite this, I love what HR stands for and what it tries to do. Following my father whose career was "personnel" in the financial sector, it was my chosen path after graduation and I enjoyed much of my first 11 years in generalist HR posts. Making a difference to individuals through my own coaching and influence and implementing structures, technology and programmes that had a profound and long-lasting positive impact on the business was hugely satisfying. Now, after a further 20 years of serving, training and supporting HR professionals from the consulting position of business psychology, executive coaching, leadership development, organisational change and 360 degree feedback, I still love HR. In fact as a business owner I long to have an HR function. The notion of having someone I trust to handle all those tricky people issues, to have an empowering yet knowledgeable listener, to have someone to reassure and build confidence where it is needed and someone to keep an eye on all legalities, processes and contracts would be simply wonderful. So let me start by expressing my heartfelt appreciation to all of you working hard to influence where you may not be fully understood, wanted or welcomed. This book has been written to help and support you in your mission so let us start by really looking at what you can promise to deliver.

My proposal is that you are the "space holder" for transformation and transition for the most magical results although there are a number of critical processes, commitments and conversations which need to be in place before you can even begin.

360 degree feedback will be explored and described in full partly because it is an intervention I have studied in great depth over the last 20 years and partly to illustrate how you can position yourself and your projects for maximum buy-in and transformation. A 360 process is a tough, hard-hitting intervention which forces employees to speak up where they are currently choosing not to. If participants (receivers of a 360 degree feedback report) are open to this feedback then they can end up having mind-blowing insights and potentially the most useful and transformational experience of their career. Yet there are many aspects to 360 degree feedback (and to HR too) that can lead the participant to being resistant which will get in the way of this potential transformation. If you can learn how to manage such an intervention with minimised resistance and unpicked upsets then you can apply these principles to other areas of HR. Let me know how you get on.

You can't change people

This is the fundamental issue underpinning the HR role. Can you change someone? You may think you can. It may seem like you do change people. Other people's behaviour shifts, people adapt to you and others are indeed open to your feedback some of the time. But people choose to behave as they do. You choose to behave as you do – you are in charge. It may feel like you are not of course. When you get upset or angry it can feel like you have no choices and you have to do what you do – but it is still you doing stuff. No one else. You might find you start behaving differently in different groups of people. For instance, you might be loud and confident at home yet quieter and more serious at work. It is as if your environment is making you be a certain way. But it is still you doing stuff. We are indeed dynamic, social creatures and our behaviour is not a simple matter, but the only person who can "change" someone else is the person themselves – either by allowing a shift to happen or by having an express intention to be different.

So, what can you do if you cannot change people? Well, what you can do is influence, guide, facilitate, enable, persuade, coach, etc. You can also create a structure or environment that makes it easy for people to shift and learn themselves. This is the easiest way forward. There are three important aspects to this enabling of change:

1. Understand the forces of resistance

We humans have many layers protecting us from outside influence and these layers can be engaged or not. In general whatever you resist persists[5], and change will not occur with any ease. "Resistance"[6] is a phenomenon studied in physics and this is seen as a hindrance to flow:

> **TRY THIS AT HOME**
> Ask someone to stand while you push them from the side. They usually topple. Then ask them to resist your force and your impact will be much less.

What can you do about this resistance? Well you can encourage people to learn the skills of managing their resistance but that is a long-term job. Best is to notice and accept others' levels of resistance and to learn how to manage these, how to minimise their impact and also how to peel back those layers. This is the approach described in the later chapters.

2. Understand how people can change

The latest in neuroscience and the world of functional magnetic resonance imaging (MRI) scanning technology is now informing us on this matter. It is clear that the brain is extraordinary in its capacity to change[7]. New pathways can be created and new messages can be generated and the key to these is practice, doing, taking action, forming habits – basically reinforcing new pathways through duplication. This requires committed action in the first place of course and new action requires exactly that – doing something new. In order to do something new an individual needs to know what to do and be prepared and willing to do it. This means therefore that the idea of a new way of doing things needs to be sold and also that it needs to be very clear exactly what the new "it" looks like.

> **EXAMPLE**
> It is much easier to take on a new way of tidying your office by knowing you should *"clear your desk at the end of every day"* rather than just thinking *"I should be tidier"*.

Key to change is the formation of new pathways, and in addition to this, structures to encourage, remind and nudge you into maintaining this new way, are critical. Otherwise the old structures, ie life as it was, will be sure to pull you back into old patterns. There are three key factors therefore required for a change to take place and be sustained:

- **Insight** – you need to have seen or learnt something fresh

- **Honesty** – telling the truth about the area is critical

- **Action** – doing something different is required

EXAMPLE

I started to manage my diary when I was working as an independent consultant and had got to be very busy in every aspect of life – balancing my life, my work, my daughter, singing, health, etc was a challenge [INSIGHT]. I looked at what needed to change and saw that I needed to think further ahead and to take more of an overview in order to then juggle the balance. The truth was I preferred to be diary driven and enjoyed being very busy but also I was not spending as much time as I wanted with friends [TRUTH]. I saw I could review the whole week on a page, once a week on Sunday and check out how it looked [ACTION] – a job that takes about 20 minutes a week.

It was great – I felt so much happier with my schedule, was able to shuffle things sometimes, plan in more time with friends, etc. It made a huge difference to every day. I have been doing this now for 15 years and my week is just not the same when I (occasionally) forget.

---

3. Know that people can change anything

Is this true? Well no, not strictly – I am tall (five feet nineish) and I may have wanted to be shorter as a child but I couldn't change that! There are two conditions we need to fulfil for this to be true:

- **You need to want to change it and see it as possible**

- **You need other people to be open to you changing it**

These conditions reflect the true and social aspect of humanity and also allow you to see that your ideas for yourself are best grounded in the reality of today's world. Anything else is fantasy!

This indicates the criticality of someone's motivation to shift, and also the requirement to have this intention integrated into life.

You can be an agent of transformation

What can you do then if you cannot change people? You can be an agent of change in so many ways and can really make a profound impact on any organisation should there be certain conditions in place. Your role in HR is a unique one – it is often not clear what your accountability is or whether you are adding value, and if you said to an ordinary line manager that you were there to facilitate them changing you would not necessarily be welcomed or indeed get thanked! No wonder there are insecurities and ambiguities about the right role and place for HR. If you are doing a fine job of enabling change then you are likely to be somewhat invisible unless you position yourself in a strong way. Selling yourself and your value is a whole challenge in itself. Who are you an agent of change for is also a key question? Each line manager? Each employee? The board? The shareholders? The CEO? All of these? Best to be clear though. You will find things easier if you choose one person and be sure to work to their agenda, get 100% committed to delivering what you can agree on as a goal, eg shift the culture to being a feedback culture, upgrade the leadership cadre, improve the leadership pipeline. Make sure you are inspired by the goal, whatever it is, and clarify current status, gather today's metrics, agree a target and get to work. Now you know what you are working towards, and who you are working for, you just need a plan to influence and enable a change... Simple!

There are four key ways you can be an effective agent of change as an HR professional – you can use just one or many of the following at the same time:

1. You can persuade and sell the new way

Sales skills are so useful! Look at what your target people really want, what truly motivates them, and speak to these. Present the benefits of the new way by positioning them clearly – you might need to present the long-term advantages, how their jobs will be easier or more fun. Alternatively you can make the consequences clear, play to their fears and concerns and tick off all their issues.

The easiest way to sell an idea is to look at what it would take to have the other person inspired and engaged. Keep trying to present your messages until such time as you get an *"Oh yes! That sounds great"* reaction. Practise on the easier ones first. Play the politics by talking to people in a strategic order.

2. You can be a mirror[8] and reflect back to people what you see

This is a remarkable technique which takes some courage but can cause miraculous U-turns. This is a key and critical part of every detailed feedback session, eg talking through the results from a development centre, and of course this is what a 360 degree feedback report does in buckets. You can use data or you can simply use your listening and your observations.

> **EXAMPLE**
>
> My husband came back from a course complaining that the leader had said that you could change things simply by repeating back exactly what you have heard to someone. He, being a mathematician and somewhat unsophisticated in the realm of handling people (just my opinion I admit), thought this was rubbish and could not possibly be true. He was quite cross about this. I listened hard and repeated back every word he had said. I watched him totally relax and look happy and I asked him how he felt about that issue now. He said, *"What issue?"* I rest my case.

The power of your listening is unbelievable. You can have the trust of every employee and listen like no one else in the organisation so take care what you do with this! All you need is to tell the truth and to pick your time and positioning to get a result. Data can really help you through and there are many types of data options: surveys, benchmark comparisons, assessments, psychometrics, 360 degree feedbacks, others' feedback, etc.

3. You can encourage critical conversations

You can direct and encourage employees to have conversations by providing processes and tools to support key people management stages. Good examples are the performance management/ appraisal steps, development planning, identifying potential assessments, hiring conversations, employee reviews, defining competencies and crucial behaviours, visioning the best behaviours, understanding the culture, etc. By guiding these conversations you are setting the scene for transformation to occur.

Alongside this the skills deployed in these conversations are key and will critically impact the usefulness of these processes. The ability to give feedback, tackle tricky subjects and be emotionally mature to take feedback all need to be monitored and nurtured. Full training is usually required (and is another initiative for you to sell in!).

In addition to setting the scene and a partial structure you can formally (or informally) mediate to ensure useful conversations occur. You can be in the room with a line manager and employee and ease the path of open and forgiving communication that will result in a new working relationship.

> **EXAMPLE**
>
> In HR I faced the challenge of helping a manager deal with a team not getting on with a man who, after a break, had returned as a woman. The team were struggling to handle their reactions and emotions. The employee in question was feeling self-conscious, awkward and victimised. There was ugly conflict and upset people everywhere. I mediated a conversation between the key parties who had been unable to speak properly and openly to each other. I asked both parties if they were willing to let something go and a solution emerged.

4. You can have crucial conversations[9] yourself

Again your power is your voice, and critical is a foundation of integrity for your voice to count and make a difference. Check that you have done what you said you were going to have done. Check that you know these people and that they know what your intention is in relation to them and that they trust you in that role. If any of that is missing or not clear then work to clear the space first of all.

Once you know you have integrity then you can start to have conversations designed to make a difference. First get clear what you really want from the relationship and what you really are after in the bigger picture. Be clear what you want in terms of the quality of relationship with that person. There are then a number of approaches you can take:

- Speak the truth, from your heart – though carefully and in a considered fashion.

- Make sure the other person is safe and their key needs are met – particularly in terms of privacy and control. Confirm confidentiality and only make suggestions, not give directions.

- Manage your boundaries powerfully – check where you have permission to talk and where you are not welcome. Stepping over these boundaries will lead to unnecessary resistance.

- Use the opportunities as they present – look out and wait for examples to occur and then make your move. Sometimes patience is best! Using in-the-moment situations is much more effective and safer than referring back to something now forgotten.

Designing interventions for transformation

There are some critical aspects of your organisation that you can clearly see could do with improvement. You listen to people, you can see the metrics, you are immersed in the people aspects of the organisation and you know that there are behaviours going on that are destructive. There are things being done and said that are not helping the general cause and performance, there are dynamics at play that are dysfunctional. If none of this is true then there are certainly things that could be done better. There always is another level to go of course, but check out how inspired you are in this mission. Check out how committed the organisation is and exactly who is committed to what and why. This clarity, if you can get it, is the first crucial step in the design of a transformational HR intervention.

First though, what is an "intervention for transformation"? Let me define what I mean by transformation – a newish term that is frequently used these days on reality TV programmes. Usually you start with a rather less than ordinary example of, say, a room or a shop or a hotel, and after a process that tends to involve an expert attempting to listen to the owner about wishes and needs, this expert follows up by magically cooking up a design, plan or strategy and then presenting it to the owner. The work gets done with various crises and traumas and tight deadlines and then everyone waits for the owner to be shown the "transformed" result with the expected tears/joy/outrage.

There may also be a big dose of coaching the owner on the inadequacy of their approach and attitude when their laziness or lack of commitment gets confronted. All good entertainment of course but in HR (unless I am mistaken) I do not think entertainment is our key objective, nor are HR seen as the "experts" in their organisations – inevitably the real valued experts will be in key business critical line roles... so we cannot use the same methods. What does all this tell us about transformational interventions?

- Transformation[10] is a dramatic shift, not a small step adjustment – it indicates that the end result looks remarkably different from the status beforehand. In the physical world there are many examples of transformation[11]:

- There is an aspect of drama and crisis in transformation – it occurs when a very different and new process or energy has been applied to something or someone, leading to the new result. The process is by its nature somewhat un-tested and un-trialled – if it had been done before in the exact, same circumstances then it wouldn't be transformational[12].

- There is inevitable risk as the end-point cannot be fully predicted. It can end up quite different from expectations and can therefore be highly disappointing. On the other hand it can result in happy surprise and delight.

- The process may not be fully understood. People do not have to be fully conscious of each part of the process for the result to occur. If people give permission for the process to occur then it can feel like it happens without them, or without their control. This can feel scary.

- Trusting the process and the leader of the process is critical otherwise the transformation will be resisted and the process will inevitably fail.

- Transformation can happen without being planned but we are talking about a planned "intervention" where there is a clear goal in mind. There are boundaries around the process and there is a planned process and strategy. Examples of HR interventions range from simple conversations or positions (on, for example, who should be appointed next CEO), to one-off simulations or practices with line managers to show a new approach, or to innovative development programmes aligned with a broader transformational goal.

There are two key steps to the design of a transformational intervention:

STEP 1: Get clear on your intentions
Clarify your primary objective and your secondary objectives

> **EXAMPLE**
>
> You want to improve the feedback and people-management skills of your middle managers. Your primary objective might be the feedback skills (on the basis that the CEO is keen on this and also you can see that if this improves, the rest may follow). Other objectives may be that you want to energise and challenge this group of leaders, and you want to improve the innovation and culture of the organisation – you want it to shift from being a little rigid and slow-moving to being more agile.

You can see from this example how easy it is to have a long checklist of things you want an intervention to do! This is a common pitfall! If you do not get clear on a priority order then you are likely to fail. In addition, if you do not get alignment on these priorities you will be seen as failing even if, according to your purpose, you are not! A useful question to ask yourself and your key stakeholders is:

> *"What is the crucial behaviour that,*
> *if we made a positive difference in this area,*
> *would impact all the other areas we want to improve?"*

How are you supposed to know what the crucial priority should be? This is not easy. The key point here is that the start of your intervention is a process where you look to discover what this is. This process of research, exploration or enquiry IS the transformation – you might call it action research[13] [14] or consultation or diagnosis. Call it whatever would be best. Sometimes it is best to wrap the enquiry into the main body of the intervention without others realising.

Once you are clear, you need a vision of the future and a clarity on what success in this area might look like. Painting this picture vividly and having it known and understood by key leaders is also crucial as it brings the future towards you.

Any intervention needs commitment and buy-in and cannot work without it, so how do you get the support you need?

STEP 2: Design your intervention
Critical here is knowing that you will get the support and a solution that will work if you design it with your stakeholders

You know what your priority objective is and have a vision for the future. There may be very many different ways of getting there so this is the time to be creative and courageous and work with some selected champions[15]. First work out what they are committed to and what they want from an intervention – listen hard, question carefully and check understanding. No need to challenge, just hear where they are – start with the key stakeholder and identify with that individual who else should be considered stakeholders. Get their wish lists, and ask them to prioritise so you know what their primary objective is too.

> **EXAMPLE**
>
> Your CEO wants changes to be managed better with less difficulty, more cross-silo working and fewer conflicts across the business. When pinned down though, the top priority is to have more productive relations at exec team level.

Now what to do? Well, consider that you can design an intervention that will obviously and visibly deliver what the CEO wants and fulfil your primary objectives at the same time. That is the trick… to work out how, first review some of the possible options:

- Building a competency framework
- Individual performance coaching
- Relationship coaching
- Team building
- Team coaching/facilitation
- Team assessment
- Observation of individuals, meetings, teams
- Assessment of culture
- Assessment of personal talents
- Assessment of style across a team
- Assessment of individual potential
- Training in specific skills and/or knowledge
- Training/briefing on new HR processes
- Introduction or adjustment to performance management processes
- Introduction of Talent review processes
- Transformational workshops on specific distinctions
- Appreciative enquiry
- Leadership development programmes
- Survey of employee engagement
- Survey of employee satisfaction
- Assessment centres
- Simulation assessments
- Business games
- Real live business projects
- Action learning sets
- Action research
- Well-known experts giving sessions
- 360 degree feedback processes
- Career development programme
- Director-level development programme
- Assessment comparing to benchmark data
- Regular reviews with a team/ individual where a pertinent question is raised
- Action research project
- Co-operative enquiry project
- World café sessions

And there are more of course... each option having advantages and disadvantages and leading to different types of experience for participants, different costs and a different type of behavioural focus. All of these require a level of expertise to design and deliver them, so the best first step is likely to be to find some experts to discuss them with and work out what might be possible. Choose someone to work with to design an intervention, check it will satisfy your objectives and plan to pilot before full implementation.

Budget will often be a source of concern for HR – not surprisingly given you are rarely in a position of generating income but only spending direct from the bottom-line – and as a business owner myself, I know this is a very precious line! But your requirement for budget and resource is also an advantage as nothing indicates and drives commitment more than £££s. Generate the interest and make a strong case for the investment. Your senior stakeholders can only say "no" and if they do then you can direct your energy where there is real commitment instead.

SUMMARY

Your value to the organisation can be very clear. You can make a significant difference to your organisation if you remember that you cannot change it or your employees yourself. What you can do is enable magical shifts through a clarity on focus and a supported strategy to deliver transformational interventions. This will provide an experience or force a conversation that will mean people start to see things differently and then be encouraged and reminded to act differently. If you get these simple but profound stages right and integrate them into normal work, then you can guarantee results.

One of the key things that will help you in delivering initiatives that make a difference is data.

CHAPTER 2

Using data to help you enable change

"Data is becoming the new raw material of business."

Craig Mundie
(Senior Advisor to the CEO at Microsoft)

The power of data

Data, metrics, numbers and facts are of interest to all of us if they are from a respected source and on a relevant topic. In fact they are the primary currency for many. All our work with Myers-Briggs Type Indicator® (MBTI)®, etc, shows us how some turn to facts and specifics while others are more likely to pay attention to opinion and feelings. All of it is highly useful of course, but there are many finance directors who only pay real attention to the figures. With facts comes power. Now, this is a problem for HR as people are so difficult to pin down and put numbers to but this is our opportunity to transform too.

Let us assume that you want people in your organisation to shift, then the key point here is that data can provide that trigger. Many of the interventions listed in the previous chapter include the use of data somehow. New insights are a critical part of the transformational process. How can you have insights without new data or a new view of data you already know? It is not simply that data will tell you the "truth" when you did not already know it – for there is no "truth" about a situation (as explained by Buckminster-Fuller[17]).

If there is no truth then what is the point of more data? Well, data can allow you to see a situation in technicolour/3D. Imagine you only have a traditional x-ray view of your organisation plus a heap of your own opinions and others too. Let's imagine you gather some additional data by taking a closer look, using new diagnostic measures, paying more attention, looking for patterns and anomalies – a bit like getting an MRI[18] scan. You will inevitably see a lot more detail. You may start to see how things connect and link and you may start to understand it better. So will your employees if they choose to look!

New data can give you a fresh perspective, as you may be viewing the organisation using new distinctions or models. A fresh perspective can lead to a whole new way of thinking – just as the spotting of a second face below can change your perspective:

Fresh data can allow you to compare within your organisation. You can compare between individuals or between teams or business units and you can compare your organisation with outside – either within your industry or broader – all depending on availability and quality of data of course. With data you can set standards and clarify expectations and you can describe what is possible. You can use it to monitor and manage processes, tracking where the breakdowns or bottlenecks are and where you are on target or off.

A grounded understanding of what is so, of what is currently real, is a critical bedrock of transformation. Transformation or development based on a false understanding of reality tends not to go too well...

Only some types of data work

Any old data is not going to necessarily work. In fact, poorly chosen and constructed data can undermine your position and ability to influence very quickly. Every HR department should have easy access to a statistician to guide use and management of data to ensure the following criteria are fulfilled:

1. Reliability[19]

If this data was gathered a second time, would the answers look the same (or close enough to count as the same)? Sometimes you can genuinely test this but usually you can only gather the data once, so you have to rely on other ways to ensure reliability. The British Psychological Society have rigorous methods of evaluating reliability of psychometrics but other sources of data such as 360 degree feedbacks may not be monitored without special attention.

2. Validity[20]

This is referring to whether the data truly measures what it says it does. There are different forms of validity – face, content, construct and criterion-related.

Face validity is a critical one and perhaps the easiest to assess by HR – this can be checked by truly listening to the feedback from participants. Do they think this relevant to them and their jobs? Does this sound of interest? Is the language right for them? Does the whole look and feel inspire and motivate those you need to engage? If you are not really sure it does all these things then you can keep working on it until it does. Critical therefore is the right level of input and consultation in the design stage. Co-creation is the ideal process to ensure you get full face validity. Face validity is the most poignant and obvious to deal with but be wary of the other forms – just because a process looks like it covers the right stuff in a compelling way still does not mean the process is accurately measuring what you are wanting it to measure.

Content validity, also called logical validity, refers to the degree to which the items of a questionnaire or test represent all facets of a given social construct[21]. For example, an IQ questionnaire should cover all aspects of intelligence. Recognised subject experts make this assessment based on their subjective judgment.

Construct validity refers to the degree to which the test measures the construct that it claims to measure[22]. This is determined statistically by the relationships between the test and measures of other constructs, and requires empirical and theoretical support for the construct interpretation. For example, the extent to which a test that claims to measure IQ actually measures intelligence, and not something else, such as motivation.

Criterion-related refers to how well the assessment predicts an outcome based on information from other sources generally considered as valid, dependable measures. Concurrent validity is distinct from predictive validity where concurrent refers to validation by a comparison with a currently existing criterion and predictive refers to the degree to which an assessment accurately predicts a criterion that will occur in the future

3. Credibility

Your data has no value to the organisation if the source is not seen as credible. This leads you to aim to reference well-established sources of research, business schools, *Harvard Business Review*, etc. You can use well-respected consultants to add credibility to data or diagnostics too. Brand comes in here as useful and you can soon test out which brands will land well with your stakeholders.

4. Opinions

Opinions matter – a lot! Opinions about an individual or about a business can make or break them – whether they are fair and just or not. So data can simply be an analysis of opinion and the same rules apply to this type of data. The numbers need to be carefully represented and the sources need to be credible to be believed. All of this can be achieved with a well-constructed 360 degree feedback tool which will then provide an all-round perspective but of course you can use opinions in many other ways and forms.

In addition to all these factors your measures are best if they are also future focused. Your priorities are looking to the future (I hope!) so it is important that your data is looking at what is likely to come, what the potential is going to be or, if it is only looking at today, that it is looking at those aspects of culture or behaviour that are desired for the future. No one is in the business of crystal-ball gazing of course, so how can anyone really know where things are going and what is going to be required in the future? Nevertheless, you can take this enquiry on yourself and can look outside your organisation, your industry and even your country for some clues.

Today's data is at the cusp of past and future – it can only represent today at best measuring what is considered today as important in the future. Given the limitations it is therefore very important to do what you can to keep it future focused. You can be sure you keep a process, programme or framework current by clarifying the shelf-life and building in review or update points. Not many competency frameworks feel fully current two years after they are constructed. This is tricky if such processes take years to build!

You can also be sure to maximise the visionary dimension by truly listening to the future strategy and the visionaries of the organisation, seeking out trends in the market-place – in your industry and in HR in general and by looking internationally, eg using the thought that the US trends may take a while to get to the UK. Be wary of past "myths" that may not now hold true. You can get swallowed into accepted thinking and practice if you are not careful.

What data does not do

Data does not have any meaning or significance in itself. Facts and/or figures are just that – facts and figures. A specific figure, eg 4 out of 5 on a 5-point rating scale where 4 is defined as "good", might reasonably be considered to mean that this person is rated as "good" on this criteria. Well yes, and no! And what does "good" mean anyhow? If a reviewer tended to rate rather generously and generally give 5s and just a few 4s, then their "4" may not mean they are all that impressed. Why would someone use the rating scale like that?

Well, there is much evidence on rating tendencies and it is very clear that there are a number of significant tendencies:

Positive rating	Rating very highly without using the full range available
Negative rating	Rating low, again without using the full range available
Central tendency or Straight Ticket error	Selecting an average rating without considering each aspect throughout the performance evaluation period
Recency effect	The most recent performance is considered while the past events are neglected
Comparison effect	Ratings are based on comparisons instead of true performance
Expectation impact	Ratings impacted by comparison and reference to expectations that may be role or individual-specific
Stereotypic tendencies	A member of a certain group is rated the same performance as the performance of the group because of common traits
Similar-to-me effect or frames of reference	Personal experience of the reviewer affects our response
Attribution bias	Errors made when people are searching for reasons to explain others' behaviour when in fact they may have no evidence
Unconscious bias	The attribution of particular qualities to a member of certain social groups which occurs through personal experience and learned cultural associations
Social desirability bias	People have a tendency to answer questions in a manner that will be viewed favourably by others which leads to an overrating of desirable behaviours

to name but a few!

In 360 degree feedback there are other tendencies that can creep into the data too:

Playing politics	Using the 360 degree feedback ratings to make a point or emphasise a weakness for political gains
Looking good	Under-rating yourself for instance to avoid ending up with others rating you lower
Fear of reprisal or reaction	Raters may be afraid of reactions so hesitate to fully express their negative views
Halo effect	Excellent performance in one aspect overshadows review of performance in other areas
Horns effect	Poor performance in one area overshadows the review of performance in other areas
First impression or primacy effect	First impression leaves a heavy influence on the assessment of performance
Attractiveness effect	A specific form of halo effect, attractiveness can affect perceptions of success, intelligence and personality
Low tolerance error	Giving poor rating to everyone because of personal high standards
High tolerance error	Giving high rating to everyone because of generalised 'good will'

So with all of these possibilities ratings can hardly be taken as definitive. A "4" could mean poor or fantastic! Other types of data may be more clear and easy to pin down, eg number of internal applicants for leadership recruitment. If it is 10 applicants for five roles then that is clear? But as soon as you get into the detail and full context of such a number you realise that a number of factors come into play, eg people may or may not have been invited to apply, the quality of applicant might vary, the types of roles coming up might be very specialist, applicants may be put off after initial enquiries. You tend to have to deal with the issue of whether that is a good or bad figure but, as this whole book is attempting to describe, it is all contextual.

There are two significant issues in relation to people data:

1.   **Interpretation** – what is this data actually saying?

2.   **So what** – what does this data mean should be done?

This is all very difficult. Gathering meaningful data can be hard work and then you might not be able to conclude anything useful from it! But there is this other big tendency called the observer effect[23] which applies to the gathering of data and leads to the phenomenon described as "what you measure is what you get". The fact is that asking questions and gathering data makes a difference to people and their behaviour. It shifts focus, it calls attention and it trains the brain to engage on the matter. For instance, the simple activity of tracking how many words I write in each writing session of this book serves to highlight my speed and efficiency. Observing my results changes my results.

Data is just numbers and facts – a "4 rating" is a "4", "10 internal applicants" for senior roles is "10", but we, as human beings, very quickly bring a sense of meaning to them. There is generally a generic dose of "that's good" or, alternatively, "that's bad" – a judgment, assessment and opinion is formed and usually extremely quickly. It appears that it can take just nanoseconds [24] for our brains to come to some opinion about an inputting piece of information. There is an alternative reaction to data which is a "nil" response which occurs when you have no data comparison or expectation – you have a neutral position until otherwise guided into a form of judgment. This process of judging data is critical to understand, as it may require unpicking or correcting. For instance, if you manage expectations well you may avoid false or unhelpful conclusions.

What meaning you attach to your data is one very important part of the equation but the other of course is how others interpret it and where it leads them. It all requires some care and, most importantly, context, and if the data is at all complex then it benefits from a sophisticated interpretation. The key to data is to look at each piece in the context of the whole picture. The real value and interpretation comes from seeing the patterns[25] from the whole.

Patterns can be useful to spot in terms of:

- Past trends

- One piece of data compared with the other data points

- Reference to other facts and actions

- Other cultures/industries/countries

- Reference to targets

- Other similar bodies – internal to the organisation or external

- Reference to expectations

The more of its context you understand the clearer you can be as to what useful meaning can be put to a "4 rating" or "10 internal applicants". Note that it is not even that you are looking for the "correct" meaning – but the most useful or the most empowering. If you can take a sophisticated view of your data you will follow through in the most useful fashion and you will be able to help your managers interpret the data with a similar level of intelligence.

Data is useful in guiding and triggering a transformational process – it helps clarify what is the case right now and helps you track and monitor progress. It helps you and others ask enquiring questions but it does not intrinsically tell you what underlies the data and what is causing the phenomenon. Understanding why something is the way it is is one question which you will probably never answer – but you might find it interesting and very useful trying to! Working out what is possible and how on earth to facilitate this is another. This is the work of every HR professional to some extent and is specifically the realm of an OD Consultant. Given these are two impossible jobs it is no wonder there is continued debate about the value of HR! That does not mean they are not worth doing, but do equip yourself with access to expertise and support as it can be a challenging and occasionally bumpy ride!

Conditions necessary for data to cause change

Data may be wonderfully clear and accurate, from a highly credible source, highly relevant, valid and reliable. Your data may be "good" data in this way but it will not necessarily impact anyone or change anything. You just have to look at the statistics and history on the health hazards of smoking to see that data alone does virtually nothing! In the 1950s 80% of adults were smoking and the data started to come out[26] with the downsides being pretty irrefutable, yet currently one-sixth[27] are thought still to smoke. It is clear from many different forms of evidence that eating less food and taking more exercise leads to a decrease in weight yet this knowledge does not make it happen! Data is clearly not enough to influence someone to change behaviour.

Working in the area of behaviour change you can see that there are five significant features that help your data have a useful influence on people. These features are listed below. If you want to be sure your data has impact, then plan to cover them all and you will be maximising your chances.

Conditions for data to be a catalyst

1. **Respect** – sources, methods and communicators of the data need to be respected and credible. And it needs to be mutual! The message surrounding the data needs to be respectful too. There is always a good reason why things are the way they are and data delivered from this position will land much better than data combined with a general air of *"This is so bad and wrong!"*. The key is the way the listener is being considered and the opinions about them, as this will impact the willingness to hear the messages and explore the options.

2. **Make safe** – for any message to be received with openness the recipient needs to feel safe. If fear kicks in then a range of different hormonal and emotional responses are likely to follow. These may feel like they lead you to safety but they are not conducive to constructive and responsible action! In order to

deliver data safely you need to protect others' privacy as much as possible and give them control over the process. You need to make sure they can speak and you can listen to what they have to say. You need to make sure they feel safe.

3. **Time** – new information and ideas need a degree of processing. This needs time and space which you can guide, but crucially you need to make sure there is time for private processing otherwise you will only get the immediate reactions which may be protective and defensive. It is this factor that has made us very clear that managers do better receiving their 360 degree feedback reports 48 to 72 hours before the feedback coaching session. Whenever this does not happen you can see and feel the difference, and you can only be in "emotional emergency" management rather than in true coaching mode.

4. **Something is desired** – the recipient of the data needs to want something for themselves or for something they are committed to. It may be a promotion or a pay rise, it may be a new career path, or it may be as simple as a less stressful experience at work or an improved relationship with the boss. There is always something somewhere they want – even if it is that you go away! If there is nothing they want connected to the data you are delivering then the data will be irrelevant to them and not worth worrying about. If there is a strong connection then you can work with it – reminding of and presenting this connection is very useful and one of your tools.

5. **Follow-through** – for data to have real sustainable impact rather than just fresh insight, follow-through is essential. Otherwise there is this phenomenon called "forgetting"!

There may be some insights which lead to new perspectives that mean you literally see the world differently from that moment on. Many new insights do not fully translate to new behaviours or actions soon enough or for a long enough period for the new habits to get fully installed and in place with reliability. Old habits definitely die hard! A useful and motivating follow-through is therefore key. It may be in the form of a well-formed development plan, a follow-on training or coaching. It could be a daily call with a buddy, it could be an intentioned action that would serve to remind, or a commitment to re-visit the data in a year... but without follow-through of some nature people are likely to slip and return to life as it was.

The world of neuroscience has brought to light the requirements for a "fear"-free state for a full and focused understanding, comfortable exploration and learning process to occur[28]. From this perspective, David Rock has been clear that 360 degree feedback, for instance, is not conducive for constructive development given where the data can take you emotionally and mentally. This book outlines how you can ensure that 360 degree feedback can be managed despite this easy risk of an individual entering a "fear"-based response. It takes care and expertise but it can be done, and the results can then be extraordinary.

David Rock describes the SCARF[29] needs people have in relation to feedback and you can see that the conditions noted above attempt to manage and deal with these needs:

S	Status	Privacy is key here to ensuring humiliation is not overly public
C	Certainty	People really knowing what is happening with the data, who owns it, who will see it etc and knowing what the next steps are
A	Autonomy	People need to feel in control of their destiny (even though in many respects they may not be!)
R	Relatedness	People fear the data will impact their relationships so reassurance and a sense that everything is ok helps
F	Fairness	People like to know the process and other people are being fair so reassurance of consistency of process may be useful

People differ in terms of these needs. You can check out your own needs in relation to the SCARF model online[30]. If you are delivering data to an individual, see if you can guess their needs – if you cannot, then assume they have them all and ensure you manage them all carefully. The key to satisfying all the conditions listed – and the SCARF needs too – is privacy. If you can be sure people have privacy when they get and look at their data then most aspects are taken care of. Interestingly, in the world of natural childbirth[31] and also in the world of caring for the dying there is a growing awareness of the need for privacy. This is somewhat counter-intuitive as in these situations, as with highly personal data, the individual is also known to need support and help – and people who care want to give just that. But it seems the human condition has a preference for private transition. 360 degree feedback data can be seen as the death of a previously held (and loved!) self-identity, so it may be that you are dealing with a grieving process here too.

SUMMARY

Data can truly help people understand things better and can lead to useful insights, but this is only if the data is of a certain quality, efficacy and relevance. Having said that, you need to be careful how data is interpreted and understood and you also need to be careful how you deliver it for a facilitative result. People need space, time and privacy to fully take in fresh personal data and they need follow-on structures to support them moving forward. Get some great data in the right conditions though, and you can impact people significantly and easily. This is what is possible for you with 360 degree feedback, so let us look at this type of data in more detail.

CHAPTER 3

360 degree feedback data tells you so much

"I have one major rule: Everybody is right. More specifically, everybody – including me – has some important pieces of truth, and all of those pieces need to be honored, cherished, and included in a more gracious, spacious, and compassionate embrace."

Ken Wilber

360 degree feedback data is one form of data that can be used to make a difference to behaviours in organisations and to transform organisations. So, just what is 360 degree feedback data? Why is it so useful? And how is it transformational?

The all-round perspective

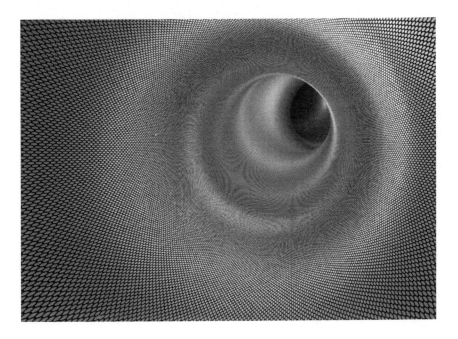

Data is described as 360 degree feedback when it is gathering ratings/ opinions from all around you in an organisation. The concept of multiple sources of data first appeared in the second world war when it is said to have been used by the German military to assess performance. It gained some traction commercially in the 1960s in the USA as part of the therapy and growth movement[32], and was starting to be implemented in the UK in the early 1990s. My first exposure to the process was in 1993 when a highly experienced and courageous OD consultant I had brought in to facilitate a team building session suggested everyone wrote the name of each team member across the top of a piece of paper with their own name at the top. They had listed the characteristics of a "top team" down the left-hand side and he then asked everyone to rate everyone else on these dimensions by passing these papers round the table. Each person ended up with a full set of clearly exposed ratings 15 minutes later and was then given an hour to consider, digest and recover! People responded in a range of ways to this experience. Emotions were high and defensiveness and justification were clear strategies of choice, but the skills of the facilitator did eventually mean that some key issues were aired and discussed that had previously been hidden. I was shocked and clear there must be a better way to do this... and I was hooked! But 360 degree feedback can indeed be done this way. Key to making data 360 is that data is gathered from a number of parties relevant to you in your job. It is usually the following categories:

Self	1
Manager	1 (or maybe 2 or 3 if appropriate)
Peers/colleagues	3-5
Reports/subordinates	3-5
External others/customers/stakeholders	3-5

It can be any number in each of these categories but it is most usually the following:

Your team/reports

Your manager

Your stakeholders

Yourself

Your customers

Your colleagues

Other 'important' people

The numbers involved and the degree of confidentiality makes a difference to how the process goes and, ultimately, makes a difference to the impact. Reviewers need to feel comfortable with the level of exposure of their feedback and ratings. This is very tricky as the feedback becomes more useful the more specific it is and the clearer the source. Just imagine getting feedback that "*someone you know thinks you are not good at listening to them and you are disrespectful and sometimes unfair – you have not got access to who this is but it is someone you know*". Compare it with "*one of the four direct reports that you wanted feedback from thinks you are not listening to them; they do not feel respected by you and think you are sometimes unfair*". You can start to consider where this is coming from, and what you might be doing to have generated this perspective. Much more empowering and useful!

This is the specificity/anonymity conundrum. The more hidden the reviewers' perspective is, the freer the reviewer will be to express themselves and the safer the whole process becomes for those giving feedback. However, feedback is of more value the clearer the source and the more specific it is. There is a line on which any 360 degree feedback can be drawn:

SPECIFICITY .... ANONYMITY

There is no right place to position your 360 degree feedback on this line but it is best to position it in line with your purpose and objective at the same time as aligning it with the permission you may (or may not) have from your reviewers. Some cultures mean that people are happy to be very open and visible in their opinions, while others really are not.

The numbers in each category is another challenge to manage. If you have one or two only in a category you are usually exposing feedback to a point. This may be OK but it may not be, so you need alternative strategies to deal with this – either by requesting approval for inclusion on that basis or by moving data across to another category to ensure confidentiality is protected as may have been promised (or, if not, expected).

Having too many in a category can also be a problem. More than five means you will get a regression to the mean[33] naturally occurring and the colour of the data will get lost among the averages. You will likely lose the subtleties in the detail. You will have more accurate averages than with fewer raters but it will be less useful in a developmental conversation. The other position to take with 360 degree feedback therefore is whether your focus is on assessment or on development and you can see there are a number of characteristics building up at both ends:

ASSESSMENT .... DEVELOPMENT	
Accuracy critical	Colour, comments useful
Lots of reviewers	Clearly identified individuals/groups
Forced choice of reviewers	Self-selection of reviewers

So, you have a number of reviewers from all around you in the organisation and they are usually asked to give you feedback, assigning ratings against behavioural statements. There may be only 40 statements they rate, there may be 100. The size of 360 degree feedback surveys has gradually decreased over the years. The average size survey for our clients is running at about 50–60 questions – a "10-minute" survey.

There may be other parts to the survey of course. These are the main sections seen:

- Ratings on behavioural statements

- Invitations for open-text feedback on behavioural statements

- Ratings on competency headings

- Invitations for open-text feedback on competency headings

- Responses to open questions

- Ranking of competencies – forcing a choice of a select number

- Ratings of importance to role

- Ratings of other observed dimensions such as values

- Ratings of other measures that can be used in research to evaluate the validity of the chosen questions and behaviours

All this data and feedback is gathered from all around you and some of it you will know already as it will fit with your own perspective and expectations and some of it you will not know. Others' perspectives will be different from your own. How this works can be shown very clearly via the Johari Window[34].

Johari Window

	Known **Me** Unknown	
Known (Others)	Agreed arena	Blind spot
Unknown (Others)	Façade	Unknown

In essence, 360 degree feedback exposes the stuff others know about you that you do not know. Just like your driving, everyone has blindspots – things you cannot see. Not because you are stupid or ignorant, but because you cannot possibly see everything. 360 degree feedback allows you to expand this box of "known arena" by showing you something of your blindspots and exposing areas you are covering up. As soon as you start to see these areas you are likely to shift perspective and start doing different things you do not see! You can only see through your own eyes, experience, expectations and standards. Others' viewpoints are inevitably different.

Whichever car you drive and however carefully you look in your side mirrors, you will always have a blindspot. Just as you will have your own view of an object like this:

In one view of this object there is a handle and it is clearly a mug, from the other there is not and it could be a pot.

Discovering what your blindspots are is supremely useful. A small but fresh glimpse of what others think of you can make a world of difference to how you handle these people in the future. You can position things differently, you can say more or less, you can choose not to deal with them at all... lots of choices!

The other opportunity for transformation comes from 360 degree feedback data exposing your facade. This is the stuff you are hiding from others or pretending about. You may portray yourself as organised and efficient to a new client for instance. After a while they may get to know you and realise you are not quite as organised as they thought and be disappointed. Delegating your organisation requirements will become a priority and you can continue the facade... but every facade brings problems and risks – there are always downsides. Just as with blindspots they are worth exposing so you can look at how you want to manage them going forward. If nothing else, you are likely to find them highly interesting!

In addition to these areas not fully known by everyone, there may be different opinions among the reviewers. In fact, there usually are discrepancies in ratings from different categories of reviewers. This again is where 360 degree feedback gets interesting. But why might ratings be different? Here are just 11 of the possible reasons behind differing ratings[35]:

1. **Degree known and observed** – how much exposure the reviewer has had makes a difference to perspective and confidence in rating

2. **Recency effect**[36] – a well-recognised phenomenon which points to the tendency for ratings to be more extreme (positive or negative) if an exposure has been recent

3. **Standards** – reviewers' standards may differ and the individual is judged against different ideas of "good" and "bad"

4. **Expectations** – expectations of an individual or a project can get created from a range of sources and can then lead to either disappointment or surprising positivity

5. **Rating tendencies** – some reviewers have a tendency to use scales in particular ways, eg on a 360 degree feedback a 1–5 scale like this:

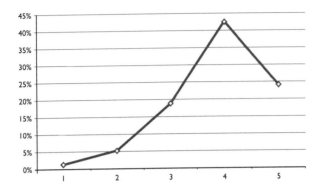

Some individuals will refuse to ever give a 5 and aim to use 1–3. Some other individuals may only give straight 5s – perhaps from a position of fear, simple adoration or straightforward non-participation

6. **Dramatic or critical experiences** – a critical incident, eg a broken promise, an angry outburst, can impact a reviewer's ratings

7. **Observations from different contexts** – different reviewers may see the individual in different settings, different teams or meetings

8. **Personal experiences** – a reviewer may have a different personal experience of the individual compared with others as their relationship may be quite different for a number of reasons (known and unknown)

9. **Stereotypic biases** – reviewers will all be rating from their own biases, some of which will be conscious and some unconscious, good and bad. These biases will inevitably impact their observations, their judgments and their ratings

10. **Personality/style dynamic** – different styles will lead to a different dynamic and relationship with an individual[37]. People show up differently with a strong extravert than they do with a strong introvert for instance

11. **Strategic rating** – reviewers may rate strategically. A common strategy is that the individual may choose to slightly underrate

themself to be sure they do not look too arrogant. Politics can enter the process and games can be played!

With so many things that can impact a rating, you might ask yourself what is the point? Well, regardless of these factors it is giving you a solid indicator of your reviewers' opinions or at least the opinions they are prepared to register right now. It is giving you a broad view of opinion so you get the whole picture – not just what your boss thinks.

What we are dealing with here is a comparison between others' opinions and your own identity[38]. Your experiences and knowledge of yourself build to form a clear self-identity. Some of us are clearer about who we are than others and getting clear can be a lifetime's journey. Wherever you are up to, though, you are attached to your identity – you are committed to it, warts and all. Otherwise you would simply change it as it is yours to mould as you wish. Our identity is so part of us that it can feel like it is us. That is how precious it is!

Now here is the key thing most do not realise – our identity has just the same range of sources of opinions as the reviewers' ratings. What you think about yourself is impacted by your cultural context, the comparisons you make, how you differ from your siblings, what standards your parents set and now your boss has set, what you are in the habit of saying to yourself, etc. Your identity is a mass of neural pathways – both positive and negative – that you choose to engage frequently. You have lots of evidence to back it up and many stories to tell to prove it. Where does this happen? 94% of studies have shown that self-reflection occurs in the medial prefrontal cortex[39] though others' views may lie elsewhere. Your whole life will have been lived inside this forming identity so of course your experience fits – why on earth would you have one that does not? You are absolutely logical and everything adds up – anything else would be discarded, ignored or forgotten (by the way, even if your identity says you are not logical, you are likely to be logical about that!). As a result of this, new data that comes along that challenges any aspect of your identity will not get an easy ride. It will be resisted at best and fought at worst. Leon Festinger[40] first identified the painful process of cognitive dissonance as being the discomfort of seeing something you did not think was true, ie where there was internal inconsistency. It is painful.

But if people are thinking different things, who is right? Good question, and the answer is no one and everyone... every perspective is valid as a perspective, everyone is as valid as the next. Each is true from their own perspective. None is "objective"[41] in the way you may be aiming for, each view being supremely "subjective"[42]. So, if views differ and no one view is "right", then what should you be aiming for? Maybe it does not matter what people think after all? In 360 degree feedback data the assumption often is that your goal is high ratings, as high as possible, across what is usually a broad range of competencies/values but maybe this is over simplistic and unrealistic. There are very few people who end up being able to deliver very high ratings across the whole picture of what is required for leadership. These are the total stars, the great all-rounders and the fabulously popular – very rare, and quite frankly, you would not wish for too many in an organisation anyhow! One view is that what there is to aim for is a high degree of alignment of the differing views from your reviewers, ie as large as possible an area of "agreed arena", ie others knowing you as you know yourself, warts and all. This fits with the general theme of "authentic leadership"[43] and certainly makes for a comfortable, freeing experience of work. Some amazing leaders have some very high ratings mixed up with some pretty low ones, and everyone knows this and their work gets organised and managed around this. Really working with your talents and managing and/or delegating the weaker areas is a great strategy!

360 gives you feedback on relevant specifics

360 degree feedback can be very general and simply be a response to wide-open questions, but it is usually designed to provide a broad picture via a collection of data on a number of specific behaviours that are deemed relevant. This process of rating specifics allows reviewers to go beyond their broad judgments and first impressions and invites them to delve into the detail of their observations. It asks them to reference their memories and search for what they have seen and heard. It helps undermine unhelpful stereotypes, makes data gathering easier and quicker and allows for an ease of collation and reporting. The specifics that are used are critical and will form the picture generated, so what should be used?

The objective is to encourage reviewers to look at and consider the behaviours they have seen and to relate to their experience of the individual so as to form a picture of their true impact. This is why many 360 degree feedback surveys are based on behavioural competency models, as seen in the example of a generic leadership model below[44].

INSPIRING LEADER COMPETENCY FRAMEWORK

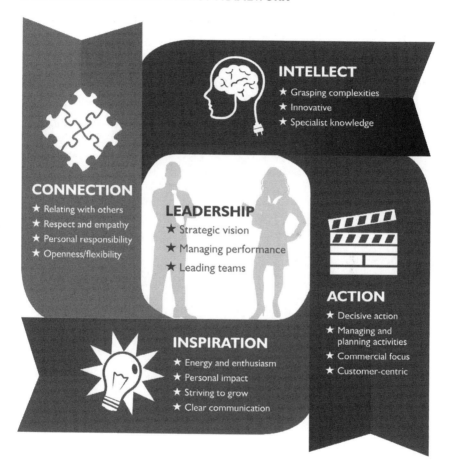

More often these days, 360 degree feedback surveys are based on value models also, although they are naturally based on behavioural translations of these values. There are generic leadership models available for use by a range of different organisations which can provide a well-tested framework and often a large database of useful comparative norm data. Most reasonably established organisations have now developed their own competency model. Some models are simple with only six competencies, and some are more complex with, say, 16 competencies and five levels!

Further examples of competency models are shown below:

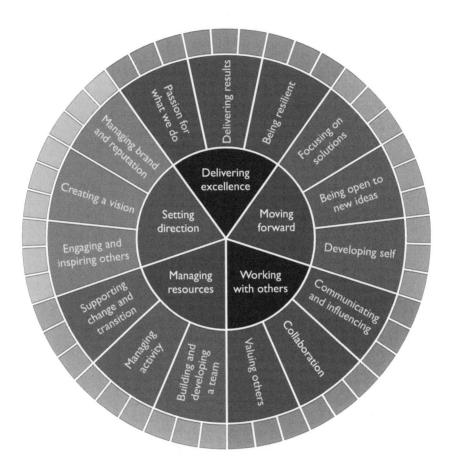

Teamwork
Living our Values
Developing Self and Others
Care and Safety
Gaining Commitment
Analysis and Decision Making
Managing Performance
Drive and Resilience
Leading Innovation
Commercial Focus
Customer Service
Teamwork
Living our Values

Some organisations have a competency framework but may not refer to the word "competency" at all, as it implies that some people may not be deemed 'competent' which has a negative feel to it. They may refer to "leadership factors' or "our DNA" instead. For the sake of consistency, however, "competency models" will be used throughout this book.

Competency models are very useful in indicating what the organisation wants to encourage and drive in terms of behaviours. They are best developed using sophisticated consultation, strategic use of data-gathering techniques[45], a dose of specialist expertise, plus a careful stakeholder-management process so that it is as visionary, valid and robust as it can be. Once developed it can be translated for a number of applications and rolled out across the full range of HR processes so that it serves to integrate all the relevant conversations and decisions. This way it sets the behavioural language and represents the future culture, and 360 degree feedback can be a useful and visible tool in this bag of tricks. This strategic and quality foundation to 360 degree feedback is essential for 360 truly to be a tool of cultural change. If your 360 is fully aligned to your other talent management processes then it will enhance, build and add value, but if it is not fully aligned it may appear slightly irrelevant and lose its power to influence and impact.

The framework you are basing your 360 degree feedback on is important but, when you are inviting feedback, it really matters what specific questions you are asking. If you ask irrelevant, unclear or distracting questions then you will get the answers you deserve, so great care should be taken to discern and decide on the content of any 360 degree feedback survey.

360 degree feedback data is just an expression of opinions

And there is no "just" about that! The very process of asking for opinions, really listening to them and attempting to understand them is a useful, transformational process. Opinion polls are well used in a number of different settings – most obviously when there is a political race to be run or a brand leadership battle to be won. And they are notoriously difficult to interpret and near impossible to use to accurately predict as they are not the real thing. The feedback the opinion polls provide, eg "the Conservatives are 5% behind Labour now for the first time this year", then feeds into the dynamic and starts to impact actions and behaviours. People work harder and voters turn out, or not.

In an organisational setting 360 degree feedback provides an opportunity that is quite unique. If you are asked to give feedback for a manager, it means they want to know your view, it can imply respect and interest, and indicate that they care about you and your opinions. When you give your ratings and your open feedback you are expressing yourself, probably a step (or even two!) beyond the level you have ever gone before. The experience is fulfilling and satisfying, even cleansing, unless there is fear entering the process, in which case there can be a confusing mix of emotions and misgivings about the process. There is the phenomenon of "reviewers' regret" which our 360 project management team has observed as some reviewers phone to ask if they can adjust their feedback now they have slept on it! (The answer is generally "yes of course" unless the "generate and email report" button has already been clicked.)

Most 360 degree feedback projects deliberately make it safe for reviewers, including the individuals themselves, to express themselves fully, although there are degrees of anonymity as noted earlier and there will be a natural level of comfortable confidentiality in this situation for every culture. Full expression may be considered dangerous or wrong, particularly in the predominantly Asian cultures where there are strong norms for what is OK to say and what is not OK. This is the paradox we are working within in 360 – we are deliberately breaking the norm with good intention (if we were not then there would be little value in it), yet norm-breaking is notoriously (and logically) uncomfortable and, should the pain get too great, it can be dismissed, dissed and outlawed. Social groups can be very powerful! You need to tread carefully and only open the feedback floodgate where you have permission and then ensure people feel safe.

The power is not just in allowing people to express their opinions, it is also in facilitating a listening beyond the norm. Most of us in HR know that listening is key and always good. You may also know that your managers are not that great at it! 360 degree feedback is designed to present data in such a way that they have to see it – but it does not guarantee that they will truly listen and it certainly does not guarantee that the reviewers will feel they have been heard. Self-expression that has not been heard ends up being quite destructive so there is a risk here. It is therefore critical that you put a process in place around and after 360 degree feedback that will facilitate this listening and truly encourage acknowledgment with reviewers.

> **EXAMPLE**
>
> A manager at an American IT company thanked me for his 360 degree feedback from three years before. He explained, *"I have been promoted and moved around the world three times since our session and I take my 360 degree feedback data with me. I put the key pages up on a slide whenever I start working with a new team and tell them 'This is who I am guys, this is what others tend to think of me, now let's work out how we can best work together!'"*

There are some key steps you can take to encourage this process of free and safe self-expression and the ideal receipt of this information. Key is information about the process – exactly why the data gathering is taking place, why them, what is in it for them, what will happen to their data, what will happen to the report and what to expect after the data has been collated. This way you are dealing with their needs for **Certainty** (the C in SCARF as noted in Chapter 2) and you are encouraging a level of personal maturity from all involved. Key to this though are the real expectations, fears and reactions of those receiving the 360 degree feedback (I will call them the "focus" for ease of reference) and you cannot control these, much as you may like to! The focus requires special and careful handling which is described in later chapters. In addition to this you cannot control what the reviewers write and how they rate. You can track them though, if you use the right system. You can monitor the time people take on their ratings and the rating patterns, and look out for anomalies. You can step in to check on their fears if you need to. You can monitor the written feedback in detail and look at taking action should comments be worded over personally or using unhelpful language (taking care to let reviewers know this will be done).

Here are a few comments from some real 360 degree feedback projects:

> *"She should stop being so Welsh!"*
>
> *"He should try wearing shirts that are not pink."*
>
> *"He really should lose weight, it would help a lot."*
>
> *"He is not a good manager but it's OK because I know he is on the redundancy list."*

If there are fears and concerns impacting the process then you could usefully intervene in some way to allay these fears. It may be a matter of asking people to trust the process and allowing them to see how it actually pans out in reality. They may only relax into the process after they have experienced the whole thing once or twice. You cannot force someone to speak when they choose not to, you can only invite and encourage and thank them for whatever level of participation they engage in. If you know for sure that however they engage in the process is just fine then they will soon get the message and relax into airing their views.

Speaking and listening cannot be forced – this is the stuff of bullying. You may really want people to hear others' views and quite probably the more you want it, the harder it will be for them to be open to hearing. But there is a lot you can do to set the boundaries, and design the content and the process to make it really easy for them to listen, as later chapters describe in detail.

Unconscious bias will underlie all the opinions expressed through a 360 degree feedback – good or bad, even if the unconscious bias is totally indifferent. This is because our opinions are fed by our unconscious, our cognitive thinking making continued reference to it[46]. You can tell if your decisions and judgments are aligned with your unconscious or not – they feel fine and clear and good, or they tend to feel awkward and wrong if they are not. It is hard to truly discern our unconscious biases as they are so hidden. Others may know more about them than you do yourself! The Implicitly bias tests[47] can show you how your deep-seated neural pathways affect the speed of your choices and processing. Test yourself and you may get a surprise! Your biases can be so easily covered up by the cultural norms of your environment that you are totally ignorant of how and why you are assessing people the way you are. You may think a particular woman talking about business is not that impressive but what part of this is your assessment of this particular woman and what part might be an unconscious bias which leads you to think women and business leadership do not go together as well as men and business leadership? You cannot tell. The problem with bias is that at the level of an individual it is impossible to tell it is happening. Yet we are always dealing with assessments of individuals and this is of course what 360 degree feedback is showing you.

360 degree feedback reflects the quality of someone's relationships rather the quality of the person

360 degree feedback data shows up at the intersection of one person and another's view of that person – in the space between them. The data represents an assessment from a person's perspective and then this data is aggregated to form the broader picture. You can see from a 360 degree feedback report how well the relationships are going and where there may be issues. It can therefore be seen as a mirror on your relationships. You can see whether in these relationships you are viewed as the gentle "pussycat" you know yourself to be, or as a scary lion.

360 degree feedback data can indicate some particular aspects of how a relationship is working. There are five areas you can easily observe:

1. **Broken agreements or promises** – where this has occurred there can be warning signs in the data or open text – especially if there are some critical questions included in the survey, eg "How well do they deliver on their promises?" which can give you direct evidence. If this is the experience of the reviewer you will likely find all their data tainted and dimmed by this issue. Worth looking out for, as those reading the report may not be aware that the consequences of these areas have been so pervasive.

2. **Wanting to be liked** – where this is strong you will spot a general positivity and a true liking by others but there may not be a wholesome respect and there may be a hint of reviewers not thinking they are being told the whole truth.

3. **Reviewers might have a grievance** – you can spot specific reviewers' issues with the focus and can look at what might underlie such an emotion. It is likely to impact all of this reviewer's ratings of course, and possibly some of the other reviewers' views too, as a dysfunctional relationship can have knock-on effects on other relationships.

4. **The focus may be depressed or in a state of severe resignation** – this you can see from looking at the self ratings and open-text comments and the comparison between these and all the other reviews.

5. **The focus may be in a significant state of denial** – they may not have heard what everyone has been saying. They may not have wanted to hear or known how to deal with it. This can be spotted when the self views are very much higher than all reviewers – especially if it is still higher after you have taken into account a potential rater tendency.

360 degree feedback paints the picture of your current leadership brand

A brand[48] is an image others have of you[49]. It is what is generated when people are given your name or when they think about you. It is the feeling, the emotion, the overall essence; it is the personality. Well this is what you can clearly see looking at a 360 degree feedback report. It often lists your highest and lowest rated behaviours from all your reviewers and this can start to show you how you are known, what you are famous for and what characteristics truly apply to you from the perspective of most reviewers. This broad-brush understanding of an individual may seem a little crude but this is the stuff that opinions are made of and therefore truly worth understanding better.

If you look at your 360 degree feedback data from afar you will see the impression you are leaving people with – just like looking at an impressionist painting:

There will of course be details within the data but you are only gathering some of those people who come across you at work so, no matter how good the instrument is, you will only have a portion of the data actually available; but, if the reviewers have been selected strategically and representatively, then the themes will tell the whole story. You can then be sure that the 360 degree feedback data is telling you what your current brand is.

The next question may be – will my brand always be exactly like this? Well yes and no. Your data and your current brand is contextual and shows how you are showing up in this culture, with this boss, doing this job, with this team, so it can be very different in different conditions and with different intentions. But there may also be strong traits and dramatic tendencies that you are likely to take anywhere and everywhere, unless you work very hard at unpicking and changing these areas. High extraversion mixed with loud, buoyant confidence could clearly be a strong trait and likely to move with you but it could land quite differently in an American sales-type environment compared to a British firm of technical experts.

Another key question is whether you can change your leadership brand should you not like it too much? Well, changing a brand image is far from easy, particularly if connected with poor integrity issues. You can see this clearly in the world of politics when some poorly considered action is uncovered and an MP, otherwise respected, feels they need to resign. Such bad marks for a brand are very hard to extinguish though it can be done with effort and support. If you want to change your brand then, following the thinking from the field of marketing, you need to change something visible and do something dramatic and then carry on in the new mode with all actions and visible signs aligned. You may also need to add in a dose of "humble pie" with a communication to key others about what you are planning to change and why.

SUMMARY

360 degree feedback data tells you lots about you – a technicolour view of your reviewers' perspectives. None of these perspectives are right and none of them are wrong, they are all valid in what they are, and together they form the broad picture. This picture is usually based around relevant factors and is attempting to provide highly specific feedback on behaviours that are all very important to the future of the organisation. These specifics are still just opinions however, and reflect the quality of your relationships and how you are currently doing in your role as well as your leadership brand, but all these angles point to one thing – this is how you are impacting others at work right now, and you (only you) did this![50]

C H A P T E R   4

Design your 360 degree feedback for pain-free success!

"If you want something new, you have to stop doing something old."

Peter F. Drucker (Consultant, Educator and Author)

So, you want to make a difference to your managers, you would like to facilitate a shift in their capabilities to manage and drive your organisation; you know data is going to help you and in particular you can see there is a useful place for a transformational 360 degree feedback tool. You just need to choose which one to use... or maybe it is not quite so easy!?

Get clear on your purpose and vision for 360 degree feedback

The first step in developing a 360 degree feedback fit for purpose is to get clear on the obvious, ie what is your purpose? A useful approach is to get clear on your primary objective, the critical thing you want the 360 to achieve. You can test out whether you have reached clarity on this by checking: *"If a year from now we had not got X, would that be OK?"*. As a 360 degree feedback project can give you a lot of things, you may of course have a "nice to have" list too which is fine. See if you can rank these priorities so you really know what is top of the list, what is second and so forth.

> **EXAMPLE**
>
> An international arts company was very good at art but not that great at management processes and the HR director wanted to develop a 360 degree feedback for general use, starting with the senior leaders. After consultation with the senior management team, it became clear that the primary objective was for the directors to take a visible action, role modelling a developmental application of their new competency model and 360 degree feedback was the chosen action.

You may have views about your primary objective but it is critical that you look at whose views you really need to be working to. First identify the other half of your 360 degree feedback "spine", ie who is as committed to this as you are[51]? Work with this person to identify who else you need on team for this project – do you need a senior leader? Is it the FD? The CEO? The HR director? Think politically and think strategically and approach your hit list starting with your favourite. Approach and have a conversation, invite them to participate in setting the strategy for 360 degree feedback and ask for their commitment if they are interested. Once you have your second team member you can then get clear who else you need on board – you might need an external expert or a strong developmental champion or a core business representative. Aiming for a core strategic team of four will give you strong, robust leadership as R Buckminster Fuller describes – the most powerful way of ensuring things happen. Once you have your four, you can agree your primary and secondary objectives with them.

Various things can happen through these stakeholder conversations. You might find there is a lack of commitment and appetite for 360 degree feedback. If this is so, do not push it. Instead work to identify with them what they are committed to. If you want to run 360 degree feedback in order to improve managerial self-awareness and also to gather data for good training needs analysis (TNA) – but no one is that keen on 360 – then check if they are interested in developing leadership skills, talk about why that might be a good idea, and look to inspire them in what may be possible if there was an increase in self-awareness. Then have a conversation about how that might best be delivered. You may then get a surprise! You may end up getting clear that there is commitment to a senior leadership programme which may of course have a 360 degree feedback as part of it!

These are crucial conversations, not to be skimped over or shied away from. A 360 degree feedback project without stakeholder commitment can be hard work and lacklustre in results. Your time is too precious to be wasting it doing that!

Once you have a core team and the primary objective is agreed, then you can start to vision what success might look like. Ask yourself what you want to be celebrating in a year's time. What does your survey look and feel like? What are your managers saying about it? What impact has it had? Who is "wowed" and by what? Write all this down and share it with your team and any others working with you to develop this tool. Visioning works best if you describe the minute-to-minute detail of a future day, with specifics in sound, taste, smell, etc. This is the way to totally fool your brain into thinking this has happened already which will then drive you naturally and easily to make it true. You do not like your world to be illogical so use logic to create it backwards!

EXAMPLE

A university in northern England wanted to introduce 360 degree feedback for all their managers (including the academics) to help facilitate a culture of feedback and open communications between managers and staff. Their vision of the 360 degree feedback was the following:

"I drive into work having dropped the kids off at school and I switch off the radio to think about my day. I have got a big meeting this morning with the vice-chancellor and six others. They asked me to present the 360 degree feedback data to them as the top 50 who had received 360 feedbacks and coaching had been raving about it and I had mentioned a few interesting stats from the data. I am feeling really nervous as I have not spoken about culture and leadership skills like this before – it is usually my boss's job. I am pleased with the prepared graphs and slides but I wonder how they are going to take it. We have all learnt so much from this exercise – some aspects are much worse than I suspected (the coaches helped me work that out) and some are reassuring but there are some useful pieces to work with. I am feeling excited and hopeful as I want to ask for a big training budget for next year as I reckon I have a good case now!

I pull into the car park and walk confidently on the slightly icy path to the HR department. I pass one of the senior academics who has been pretty anti-management but today she said hello very respectfully. Feeling good!"

The main thing to say about this form of visioning is, given how likely you are to get what you have seen, be very very careful what you wish for!

Choose your point on the "assessment:development" continuum

The reason it is so useful to identify your primary objective is that it can then dictate the position for your 360 degree feedback on the continuum between "assessment" and "development" and the appropriate design factors will then follow. Pinpoint your position and your many design choices will become very easy. As an example, when you come to decide who selects the reviewers, you are guided to say that the choice of reviewers should be validated by a key other (manager/HR) if you are at the "assessment" end, and you would go for a totally free selection if at the "development" end.

The following table indicates some of these design factors indicated in three positions – at assessment where accuracy and reliability are key, at development where individual learning is the critical outcome and half and half where learning and accuracy are equally important (and the primary objective might be "identifying training needs" for instance). Here are 21 key factors in designing a 360 degree feedback and how they differ across the continuum:

Design factor	Assessment	Development
Rating scale	4 or 5 pt	5-9 pt
Choice of framework	Generic/tested	Consult on options
Creation of questions	Use tested only	Consult widely
Testing of questions	Pre-trialled	Pilot on target group
Inclusion of developmental open questions	Not essential	Yes
Use of benchmark data	Useful if valid	Useful if perceived as valid
Size of survey	80-120 questions	40-120 questions
Inclusion of ranked data	Useful not essential	Essential
Testing of model	Essential	Useful
Number of questions per dimension	5-10	4-8
Validating of survey	Essential	Useful
Choice of reviewers	Validated/directed	Participant choice
Process of engaging participants	Directed/managed	True invitation
Look of 360 degree feedback survey and report	Clarity essential	Clarity and interest essential

Design factor	Assessment	Development
Content of report	Accurate interpretation	Accurate and engaging
Title of 360 degree feedback project	Clarity is key	Essential to be inspiring
Use of external coaches for feedback	Not essential	Adds value
Use of internal coaches	Not essential	Adds value
Briefing of reviewers	Critical	Critical
Briefing of participants	Critical	Critical to invite
Integration of 360 degree feedbacks with other HR processes	Not essential	Useful

Translate your framework into a 360 degree feedback survey

Before you look to generate your 360 degree feedback questions you need to reflect on the framework (or frameworks) you are basing them on. You may be really clear what model or framework you are using – it may be your competency model (with or without levels) and/or it may be your values, or it may be another generic model that you have chosen to adopt or integrate. Whichever way, check carefully that it is up to the job of supporting a robust 360 degree feedback. What does a framework need to have in order for 360 degree feedback to work? The following checklist gives you the five key criteria your framework needs to fulfil:

1. **Future-focus and currency** – check that your framework is truly reflecting the criteria currently considered critical for the future health and performance of the organisation.

    Solution: It may need updating or refining or it may be that it is time for a full refresh[52]. If you do not have the time or appetite then simply find a generic model that feels more relevant and develop a map across to your own model. Simple!

2.   **Specificity of dimensions** – it is easy to have broadly defined dimensions, eg "Leadership" or "One Team". They sound great and can give clear messages about what is important but if they are too broad they will not work in a 360 degree feedback. If they are broad they will need a large number of questions to properly cover them, eg "leadership" would likely require at least 12 questions to cover the key aspects. Twelve is too many as people struggle to understand that many at one time [53] and also because within the 12 there will likely be some behaviours that work antagonistically with others, eg "inspiring others" will work somewhat against "clarifies standards of performance" (meaning that those individuals who are great at one will, statistically, be likely to be not so great at the other). Antagonistic behaviours in one dimension will make for bland and misleading data at average and dimension levels and therefore lead to a confusing report.

Solution: If you have broad dimensions you can fix this by breaking them into sub-categories for the purpose of your 360 degree feedback.

3.   **Differentiation between dimensions** – dimensions can easily overlap, eg "team oriented" and "positive relations" are not quite the same but could overlap, depending on the definitions and the detail within.

Solution: For 360 degree feedback you need to pull them apart and make sure the questions are not increasing the overlap and leading to more confusion and double-counting than is already occurring.

4.   **Breadth of whole framework** – your framework may not cover the whole of what is relevant for the specific purpose of your 360 degree feedback. This can often occur if you are wanting to use your company competency model and aiming to do 360 degree feedback for senior leaders' development. An organisation-wide model will not cover everything relevant to senior leaders' work. It may well be missing key aspects that are required in the managing of managers, driving organisational changes and the culture and it may not include sufficient strategic, long-term or political aspects of leadership.

Solution: You can look to add additional pieces to your model –
it may be simply two or three extra competencies or dimensions
with a suitable label or providing extras to choose from. This way
you get the coverage you need and you are still using your model.

5. **Number of dimensions** – your framework may be very detailed
    (with say 15 to 24 dimensions) or very sparse or broad (with, say,
    three to seven dimensions). As you can tell from these numbers the
    most useable number of dimensions to work with for 360 degree
    feedback is 8 to 14.

    Solution: If you have too many you can bundle them to form
    fewer and if you have too few you can create sub-categories,
    although you may instead decide to use the structure of a generic
    model that really works and map it across to yours as this way the
    structure and number in yours does not impact the workability of
    the 360 degree feedback.

Once you are clear on the framework you then decide how long you
want the survey to be – is it a 10-minute rating completion (plus flexible
open-text commentary) or a 20-minute survey, or longer? If you write
your questions using the Talent Innovations style then 50 questions in 10
minutes is the simple equation[54]. Key to this is not just the matter of time
taken by managers to complete their surveys, it is also important to be sure
you have the right number of questions per dimension being measured, eg
if you have 12 competencies and it is a developmental purpose, then you
might aim for five questions per competency; if assessment, you might aim
for six or seven per dimension – to get a higher level of accuracy.

Let us assume that you know which dimensions, you have their definitions
and any supporting material or data on behavioural indicators. You may
then need to consult and gather data in order to be sure you are including
the most relevant examples and observable behaviours. You may wish
to consult widely to gain more support and commitment and ideas from
your target managers and/or your stakeholders. This is when techniques
such as focus groups, visionary interviews, critical incident interviews and
repertory grid interviews come in very useful[55]. You may also want to refer
to generic instruments to borrow ideas and benchmarked questions.

Crafting questions (or "**items**" as we call them in the 360 degree feedback trade) is the next stage. This needs to follow strict guidelines and standards in order to be sure they are going to work:

- Be simple and easy to understand – no flowery concepts, easy to apply to anyone. Ask yourself *"Do I see these people doing this?"*

- Standard English (or International English if appropriate) – so it can be understood by every reviewer who may be asked to complete a survey. You may need to provide translations.

- Only one behaviour at a time, not two and not three – eg if you ask *"How well does he plan resources so the team can achieve high standards of performance?"* you are asking about planning, organising of resources, managing of the team and setting of standards. This is four questions. All may be relevant but a low rating on this item will leave the focus confused about what they have to do more or less of.

- Short – the more people have to read, the longer and harder the process and the more complaints you will get. We aim for four to seven words in a question. Avoid duplication – even repeating an interesting colourful word in a different item can feel like duplication to a reviewer so only use words like 'external stakeholder' once if you possibly can.

Following these guidelines, let us say you now have your drafted items. You may want to consult on these. You can use this to bring people into your project but take care not to let them argue too long. What works is for you to hold firmly on to the integrity of the instrument and the construction of the survey. Others can mess with the detail within as long as they do not break the rules above. Promising that you will listen to all feedback and then take a judgment on what would work best for everyone is a useful approach.

You then need to decide on your rating scale and the formation of the survey. Rating scales are very tricky and can get quite political too. You might need to be aligned to another rating scale used in the organisation, eg your appraisal scale, or indeed you might need it to be very different from this. Take advice[56] and pilot[57] it, whatever you do. Our favourite rating scale is the following:

Understanding the Rating Scale

When you see values in the remainder of the report, they are based on the following numerical meaning of the scale used in the questionnaire:

1	2	3	4	5
Poor	Fair	Satisfactory	Good	Excellent

With this scale the survey may look like this:

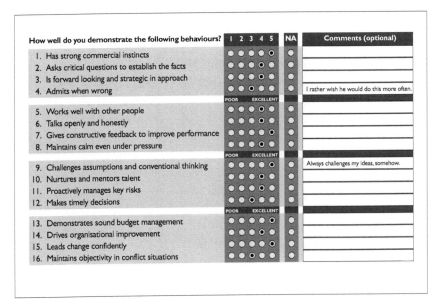

If you use the same scale as a generic instrument such as this one you will then have the opportunity to refer to the benchmark data.

Look at mixing ratings with open-text questions. These are our favourite open-text questions:

Please answer these questions:	
1. What do you think you are particularly good at?	
2. What are you currently working on to improve?	
3. What obstacles do you have in your learning?	
4. How can you increase your current effectiveness?	
5. What should you work on to assist your career in the future?	
6. How can the company better support your growth and development?	

Look also at including a ranking survey or a "forced-choice" section where you might, for instance, show all your dimension headings and ask people to rate which two or three are strongest for this person and which two or three are weakest. This allows you to be sure that every participant will get colourful data, regardless of how bad or good they are generally. It also provides participants with a very interesting insight on how people really feel about them and gives more evidence of their leadership brand. Here is an example of how this might look in a survey:

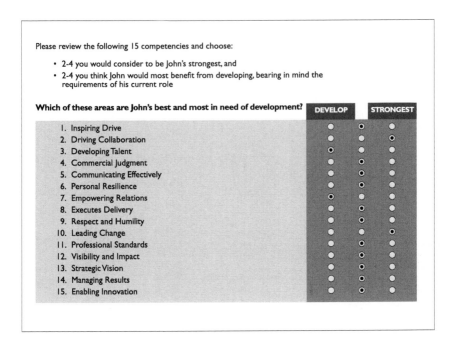

Please review the following 15 competencies and choose:

- 2-4 you would consider to be John's strongest, and
- 2-4 you think John would most benefit from developing, bearing in mind the requirements of his current role

Which of these areas are John's best and most in need of development?

	DEVELOP		STRONGEST
1. Inspiring Drive	○	◉	●
2. Driving Collaboration	○	●	◉
3. Developing Talent	◉	○	●
4. Commercial Judgment	○	◉	●
5. Communicating Effectively	○	◉	●
6. Personal Resilience	○	◉	●
7. Empowering Relations	◉	○	●
8. Executes Delivery	○	◉	●
9. Respect and Humility	○	◉	●
10. Leading Change	○	●	◉
11. Professional Standards	○	◉	●
12. Visibility and Impact	○	◉	●
13. Strategic Vision	○	◉	●
14. Managing Results	○	◉	●
15. Enabling Innovation	○	◉	●

You may also wish to add some extras – some measures that you might want to use for research and validation purposes only. We call these "hard measures" which are extremely useful for checking that your competency model is truly reflecting those behaviours that relate to effective leadership and can tell you which of your items are the real career drivers. Here is an example set:

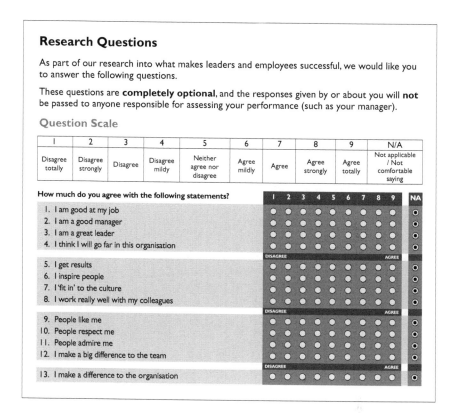

Design every web page and communication on brand

If you are clear what your purpose and vision is for your 360 degree feedback then you will likely know what will be the best "feel" and what the key messages should be. Take time to consider this strategically – just like with a business brand – and the detail will follow easily. The following case study shows you how it can be done:

EXAMPLE

A London-based international insurance company had used 360 degree feedback before, with managers using it as a standalone appraisal tool. It had a lacklustre reputation and was not viewed as high impact or high value but simply a necessary part of management. They were launching a development programme for their top talent and wanted a 360 degree feedback designed to be integrated into the process. They wanted an energising, motivating, high-impact experience with a relevant and inspiring feel. Their vision was, in fact, that other managers outside this group were queuing up to use their tool! They decided to use the HR branding plus a stroke of purple and blue which they were using on all the top talent materials – aligned with their training provider's brand colours. They used a graphic designer to create a sweeping swish of purple which they used in all the web pages and across all emails and other communications. The 360 degree feedback web pages used the same vibrant colours and a new font. The wording used throughout was upbeat and vigorous. They were helped by input from their comms team, had a signed statement from the HR director and professionally designed graphics at every opportunity.

The content of the survey was piloted carefully so as to be sure the most impressive behaviours were included as well as the core company values and competencies so all objectives could be met. The title of the instrument was discussed with key parties and "**In the Know**" was the chosen heading for this 360 degree feedback with no particular mention of 360! The report front and back covers were designed by the marketing department and the data within was coloured in the brand colours and top talent font too! The participants from around the globe were briefed via email, information packs and finally a special series of webinars where their questions could be answered. Finally, the reports were carefully printed and bound by the supplier and distributed to the coaches before the sessions as well as emailed to the participants. The reports were received with quite a "wow" and the developmental exploration had a feel of energy from the start.

Design your 360 degree feedback output on brand

Your 360 degree feedback report is a document like no other. It is received with anticipation or even trepidation and it is read eagerly and/or nervously. Emotions emerge ranging from relief to shock and anger and then stuff happens... it is no wonder it gets remembered! I can still see the page which had some feedback written in my 360 degree feedback 12 years ago – it said *"She is great and really scary"*. I had no idea how or why and was quite perturbed by this comment. It took me a few months to work out and this report is still in my file of precious/personal items along with my early CVs, my degree certificates and my very first occupational personality questionnaire and Myers Briggs profiles! So it needs to look good!

You know what adjectives your 360 degree feedback project needs to fulfil by now – it may be inspiring, challenging, amusing, lighthearted or seriously professional and profound. List them and agree them with your stakeholders. Check they still fit the whole purpose and context and ask yourself what the 360 degree feedback report should look like given these adjectives. A professional, clear, quality and data-focused report can look quite different from a fun, exciting and thought-provoking one.

Give lots of attention to the front cover and potentially the back cover as well as the binding. The packaging makes a difference and sells it appropriately. Make sure it fits your adjectives, your HR branding and your culture as it will do more good if it fits within the norms. You can normally assume coloured, bound reports with a reasonably professional looking front cover work as a generic starting point for most organisations. In my experience there have only been two organisations where this has been clearly wrong – at Tate (international art expertise clearly demanding another level of design!) and with an environmental community at the height of the green movement (where I was the only one who did not turn up carrying a cycling helmet). I was told I was *"Too shiny and corporate"* even though I finished my presentation in the semi-darkness of a wintry late-afternoon as there was clearly no permission to put the lights on! No doubt there have been other times too when it was not right. Your aim is to have the report land with the key stakeholders and participants with a *"Great – just right"* response.

On your front cover you need to have basic information such as project title, name of participant, numbers and types of reviewers. Consider listing the names of the reviewers – this tends to make it easier for the coach and participant to get on with understanding the data. A lot of time gets wasted trying to work out and remember whose data has reached the end point. Usually including the names does not undermine any confidentiality issues, but if it does then clearly just the numbers should be listed.

Consider your introduction and get clear what the key messages are. This can usefully be signed off by senior stakeholders. You may want to include a quote or signature from a champion or sponsor. Describe the process of 360 degree feedback, and the objectives, and clarify any rating scale that is used as well as what will follow.

Now comes the data! Once again refer to your purpose. If you want the participant to have a positive, supported learning experience then display the data in an order and method that will achieve this flow and experience as best as you can. Go with the journey that the participants' minds follow. You will only discover this flow by experience and trial and error. People tend to want to know "why" and "what for" first (hence the intro), and for reference it is useful to indicate the basis of the survey (usually your competency model) to ensure you position the credibility of the assessment. Then they want to know how they did... good, bad or indifferent? Showing them an overview first off works well – as shown here:

Competency Results

Below you will see the average score of all ratings given under each competency. The diamonds show the average rating that you have given yourself, while the bars show the average rating given by everyone else who responded.

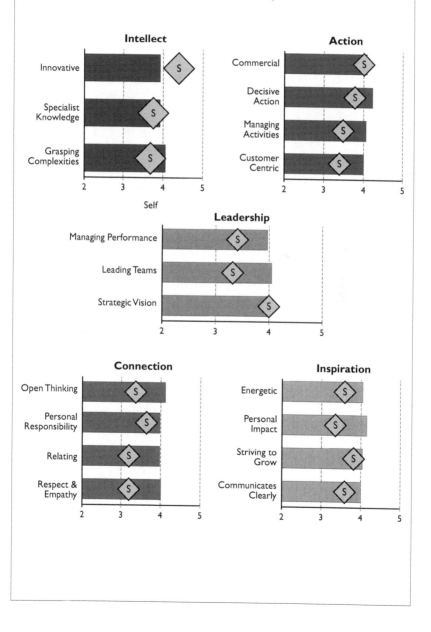

You may then want to show them an overview at a lower level of detail. Examples are shown here:

Competency Results

Below you will see the average score of all ratings given under each competency. The diamonds show the average rating that you have given yourself, while the bars show the average rating given by everyone else who responded.

Then you usually want them to see the positives and the best bits. Give them the "highlights" but make sure they really are the highlights. What works best is to display the questions rated highest by all the non-self reviewers, ie everyone else. You can compare these to the self-view if you want. If your survey is 50-items long then you only want to display four to five highlights; if it is 90-items long then six to seven can work. You do not want to mislead them. Be clear that these are the top results (regardless of the amounts).

Example: Talent Innovations' 'Inspiring Executive' highlights

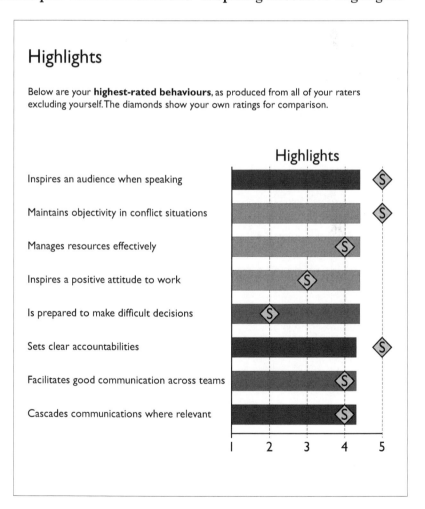

Blindspots are worth including next, eg others rating something very low when the self-rating is high. Take care with the equations underpinning the data however, as you do not want to highlight blindspots that are not real, eg mean others rating = 3.1, self-rating = 4 on a 5-point rating scale may sound like a blindspot but may not be depending on the reviewer patterns (4 may be low for the self-rating and 3.1 may not be that low for others; on the other hand, 4 may be one of the highest from the self and 3.1 may be the lowest from others, so be indicating a true difference in perspective). Again, take care not to mislead.

Example: Talent Innovations' 'Inspiring Executive' blindspots

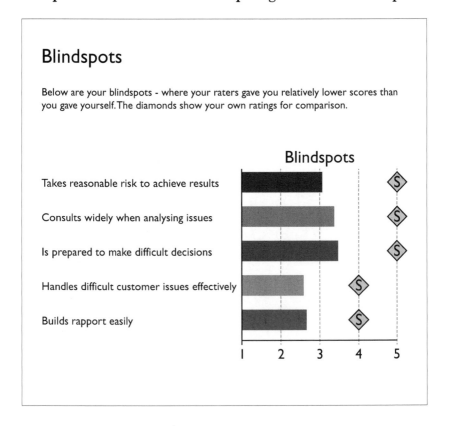

The data can then be shown in a number of different ways and, for the most accurate interpretation, all of these perspectives are worth including:

1. **Data showing the reviewer type average on each competency** – this allows you to see the overall pattern across the models and between the reviewer types, eg:

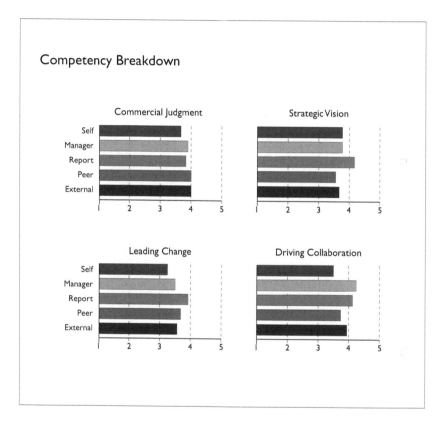

2. **Data showing the rating tendencies for each reviewer** – this allows you to spot if there are any specific outliers within a reviewer category, an essential fact to allow for accurate interpretation of the reviewer averages (eg if there are three 'colleagues' and only one rates very harshly with the other two very positive then the average for the category will imply that colleagues are lukewarm in their opinion which is now clearly wrong for all three of them!).

Understand Your Raters

The shaded blocks on these graphs illustrate the distribution of ratings for each of your selected raters. The figure in the middle of the shaded area is the average rating given by that rater.

Rater Score Distributions

3. **Norm (or benchmark) data can be shown early on too** – whether this is organisation-specific or an external set of comparative norm data. You need to consider inclusion of this data carefully and check acceptability as organisations vary in this respect. You also need to know that everyone (yes, everyone) has a question in their mind when they look at their 360 degree feedback data – the question is *"How good [or bad!] is this compared to others?"* They may not ask it out loud but they do not seem to fully process the data until they have some sort of answer. They will make it up if they have no data but you may prefer to equip them with the facts. A coach or a boss can give them a perspective on this of course, so full norm data is not necessary.

Example: Talent Innovations' 'Inspiring Leader' benchmark comparison

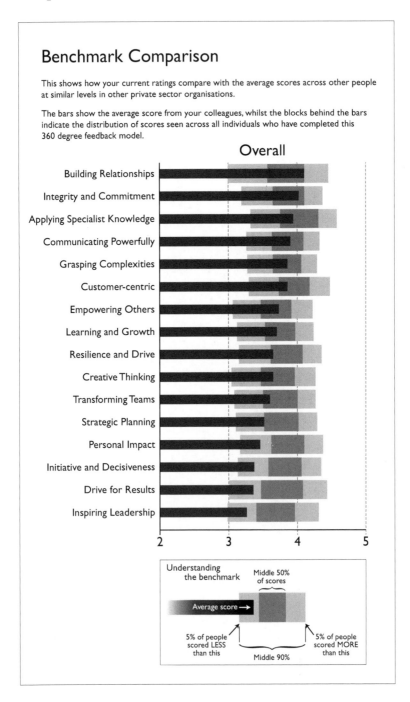

Benchmark Comparison

This shows how your current ratings compare with the average scores across other people at similar levels in other private sector organisations.

The bars show the average score from your colleagues, whilst the blocks behind the bars indicate the distribution of scores seen across all individuals who have completed this 360 degree feedback model.

Overall

Building Relationships
Integrity and Commitment
Applying Specialist Knowledge
Communicating Powerfully
Grasping Complexities
Customer-centric
Empowering Others
Learning and Growth
Resilience and Drive
Creative Thinking
Transforming Teams
Strategic Planning
Personal Impact
Initiative and Decisiveness
Drive for Results
Inspiring Leadership

2   3   4   5

Understanding the benchmark

Middle 50% of scores

Average score →

5% of people scored LESS than this

5% of people scored MORE than this

Middle 90%

Example: Company-own benchmark comparison

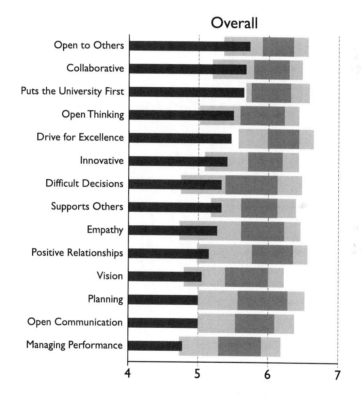

Benchmark Comparison

This shows how your current ratings compare with the average scores across other people at your level in this organisation.

The bars show the average scores you got, whilst the blocks behind the bars indicate the distribution of scores seen across all individuals who have completed this 360 degree feedback model.

Overall

- Open to Others
- Collaborative
- Puts the University First
- Open Thinking
- Drive for Excellence
- Innovative
- Difficult Decisions
- Supports Others
- Empathy
- Positive Relationships
- Vision
- Planning
- Open Communication
- Managing Performance

4   5   6   7

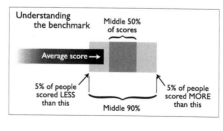

Understanding the benchmark

Middle 50% of scores

Average score →

5% of people scored LESS than this

5% of people scored MORE than this

Middle 90%

4. **The worst data can come next** – again, readers will be wanting and waiting to find out where they did worst so you may as well give them the answer sooner rather than later. [I remember inventing the term "lowlights" for this section after a trip to the hairdresser!] If you want a positive feel then you need to list fewer lowlights than highlights. The appropriate numbers could then be five highlights and four lowlights for a 50-item survey, seven highlights and five lowlights for a 90-item survey. This trick gives a positive feel regardless of the level of ratings.

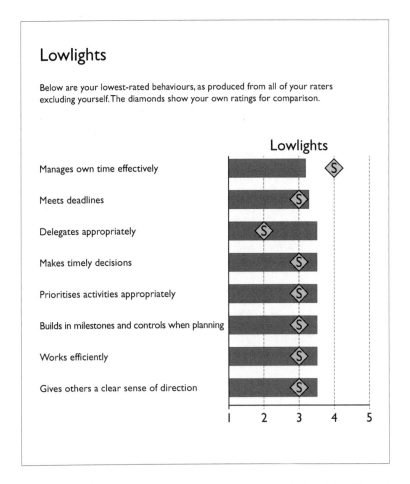

5. **The facade** can come if you want to include this although, as with the blindspots, you need to be careful with the arithmetic and interpretation.

6.   **Full detail at item level** – this is the meat of the data and can be displayed in a number of ways ranging from tables full of numbers, pages full of graphs or a mix of the two. You can also include the open-text feedback at this stage. Here are a few different examples:

Example: Talent Innovations' 'Inspiring Leader' item-level data

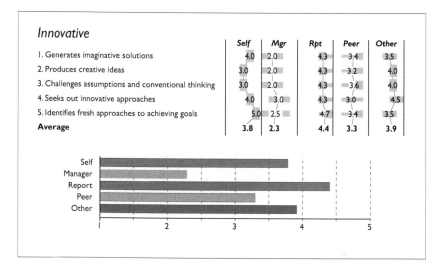

Innovative	Self	Mgr	Rpt	Peer	Other
1. Generates imaginative solutions	4.0	2.0	4.3	3.4	3.5
2. Produces creative ideas	3.0	2.0	4.3	3.2	4.0
3. Challenges assumptions and conventional thinking	3.0	2.0	4.3	3.6	4.0
4. Seeks out innovative approaches	4.0	3.0	4.3	3.0	4.5
5. Identifies fresh approaches to achieving goals	5.0	2.5	4.7	3.4	3.5
Average	**3.8**	**2.3**	**4.4**	**3.3**	**3.9**

Example: Talent Innovations' 'Inspiring Leader' item-level data simple format

Question Responses - People

Inspiring Leadership

	Self	Mgr	Cust	R/P
1. Inspires a positive attitude to work	4.0	-	4.5	3.9
2. Gives a clear sense of direction	5.0	4.0	4.5	4.0
3. Energises people to work towards goals	5.0	3.0	4.5	3.6
4. Has an inspiring vision for the future of the organisation	4.0	3.0	4.5	3.6
5. Engages others in the team goals	5.0	4.0	5.0	3.7
6. Excites people in their vision	4.0	3.0	4.0	3.4
7. Has a compelling vision for success	4.0	3.0	5.0	3.7
8. Demonstrates belief in the vision	4.0	4.0	5.0	4.0
Average	**4.4**	**3.4**	**4.6**	**3.7**

You can go horribly wrong with this data if you are not careful. Think about your audience and whether they are all going to be happiest with numbers or charts? With lots of detail or less? With more data or less? With full dense pages or more space? You know your people so simply match their needs. This part of the report can look very different if you are dealing with financial analysts in the City compared with curators at Christie's and different again with supervisors in a retail environment.

7. **Open-text feedback** – best to display this with clear headings and a formatting which accurately shows where one person's view starts and stops. You will get more value from this data if it is spread through the report and physically close to the data it is pertinent to, so the participant can look at the data and immediately get the explanation or further elaboration.

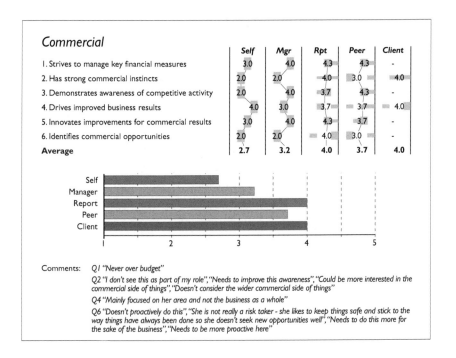

Broad open-text feedback is also really useful – as in this example:

Your reviewers have specifically said

What do you think he is particularly good at?

"Customer service, communication and negotiation."

"Supporting people."

"Being passionate about his work."

"John is attentive, understanding, and flexible and creates an environment where I can do my job effectively without 'micro managing'. He is also very politically aware and shares this regularly. Importantly he is open and very approachable. Please keep doing more of this!"

"Great at developing new ideas."

What should he work on to improve his personal effectiveness in his role?

"He could be more assertive in meeting situations. He has a lot of good ideas and leadership qualities but needs to assert himself more in that area."

"Patience."

"Be more assertive and drive the team."

"Perhaps greater exposure across the business would benefit him."

"Influencing the direction of the team."

What should he work on to assist his career in the future?

"Better awareness of team conflict, not running away from it."

"More exposure across the business."

"Good development plan."

"Put your stamp on things more."

"Visibility."

What do you think he is particularly good at in terms of displaying our Values and Core Behaviours?

"Accuracy and attention to detail."

"I think John is strong across all the company values. With respect to core behaviours, John is very accurate and attends to detail but sometimes needs to infer what information the placing team are fundamentally concerned with and what their key requirements are."

"Mainly the teamwork aspect of the values Talbot encourage along with achieving excellence through hard work."

"John is incredibly focused on detail, service and his contribution to his team, peers and the business."

"John is a very strong people person and quickly and effectively builds relationships. He is trustworthy, very committed and reliable."

"Attention to detail, approachable, good at praising others."

How can he increase his current effectiveness in order to better display our Values and Core Behaviours?

"John should consider more effective delegation and focus on more strategic matters."

"John should work on his analytical interpretation and how this interacts with taking commercial decisions and the subsequent impact on the financials."

"By considering the views of others."

"To continue to develop his skills going forward in regards to the innovations that are being implemented in the claims team."

"Liaising with the placing side of the business."

Finally, make sure you finish properly with a name and number for people to refer to if they need support (or link to resources) and include the appropriate development planning worksheets or guidance. The best approach here is to make sure that the worksheets are aligned with the programme and the 360 degree feedback process it is connected to. Some participants will complete such forms (see below) but most will not, so the follow-up support required is a whole other chapter.

Development objectives specific to your leadership style and the result of your 360 feedback

Remember to consider how you use your strengths to support your development as well as thinking about areas to improve

Development objective	Importance – business/personal level	Actions to achieve	Target date	Achievement

Personal aspirations (eg for your leadership, team, career)

Follow all these points and you will definitely have created a 360 degree feedback that a participant will find it useful to go through and you will definitely get the *"Great - just right"* response! Trial your report with a real 360 degree feedback. How it works in practice can often be quite different from what you might imagine.

SUMMARY

Designing your 360 degree feedback is a critical stage and there are literally hundreds of details to decide upon. You can aim for a fully integrated, beautiful-looking and clear report but this can take some putting together. Getting input from key personnel at the right times helps; designing for your objectives is critical and accurately translating your model into workable quality questions/items is essential. All the emails and communications then need to be written and the report can be designed. You are then ready to roll and need to consider what to do to make sure people are OK through the experience.

CHAPTER 5

The power of 360 degree feedback depends on how the individual is left

"Sometimes it's the scars that remind you that you survived. Sometimes the scars tell you that you have healed."

Ashley D. Wallisima

"No pain, no gain"... really?

A key dilemma is that 360 degree feedback is not very useful if it simply confirms everything you already knew – yet the very experience of being presented with data that gives you a new perspective, a new "truth", is tricky. Not just tricky, often painful. You are faced with a new reality and you may not like it. In fact, if the 360 degree feedback is designed to show views from all angles and give lots of different perspectives, then can almost be a guarantee that there will be new, previously unknown information emerging. And this is not like "news" – the latest information about the world at large, or the economy, or the local planning issues – it is about you personally, your reputation, your competence, your career and your future. Or so it seems!

There is a lot at stake if you allow yourself to really look at the data and this so easily means that you respond as if your very survival is at stake. Your primitive brain[58] kicks in in milliseconds and this response will protect you as if your life is being threatened and it will be highly effective. The whole process of response works very well and serves its purpose. It generates hormones and feelings and thoughts and a whole pattern of behaviour deep rooted in the past. It will feel automatic and as if there is no control. The tiny amount of brain power we have in our cognitive centre[59] does not get a look in at this stage, not for a while, yet this is the processing required to make real sense of the data and to get clear what to do. A 360 degree feedback process that has participants go to their primitive protection response will only get good results if participants somehow get through and over this response. Only then will the exploration, recalibration and learning occur. Your 360 degree feedback project is best built with the express intention of assisting and facilitating people in dealing and recovering from this emotional response should it occur. Making sure people get over their upsets is a challenge however, especially as many can get quite fond of their complaints and "position". Their upsets become part of who they are and can be further justification of why their lives are as they are. This chapter covers tips and techniques as to how to do this should there be any degree of openness to recover. But of course it is also very useful to run 360 projects with the intention of preventing this response in the first place, so let us look first at how to manage the process for prevention.

Participants need to be "OK"

360 degree feedback can be an emotional ride for participants. For some it will be no big deal, they will take it in their stride, be interested in their data, process it and emerge clear about where they need to go in terms of moving things forward. These individuals are likely to be ambitious and/or have a growth mindset[60]. There is something they want for themselves. They will be hungry for development and they will have a level of emotional maturity that supports a healthy, constructive processing of their data. All your participants may be like this, but they may not. Even the strongest, most ambitious may in fact have some hidden sensitivities even they were not aware of until they get some feedback from a respected source that surprises and disappoints them. It is safest and most responsible to plan your 360 degree feedback assuming everyone has such sensitivities, as you can then be sure you are doing your utmost for everyone to be OK.

Is it really so critical to make sure people are OK – surely those who "need" 360 degree feedback the most are those who are going to be most upset and they should just get over it. Well, the answer to this is that it depends what your objectives are for 360 degree feedback in the first place – if it is to support performance management of "problem" individuals then you are right to expect upsets and you will be prepared and happy to deal with them in the context of resolving the whole issue. If it is to encourage and enable personal development of the individuals, then upsets will not help the individual shift from the useful "insight" to action or change. Our active, conscious cognition will not be able to work out a new, easy way of behaving at work if it is busy being distracted by fear, anger or upset emotions. Not much clever stuff happens when those emotions are going on[61].

Transformation only takes place when there is the safety and comfort to explore and consider new possibilities. You need to be able to "let go" and to see what emerges – a bit like being pulled along in the current of a flowing river. While you are afraid and cautious you are standing on the bank looking at the river, but not stepping into the new.

Once you have allowed the new insight or perspective in and you have dabbled your toes in the water, you may find it is upsetting and you do not like it – this is a different and opposite riverbank of "upset" – the bank of "resistance". Getting stuck on either bank is not constructive – no learning or shifts can really take place while you are emotional or stuck.

People can be upset but if they are working in a professional environment, particularly where the norm is emotional restraint and politeness, eg in the UK, they may of course think that they should not show their upsets. However, in 360 degree feedback projects the upsets can leak out. For instance, the initial emotions can be seen by others when they would not normally be so exposed and this can totally undermine the process and the status of the individual participant. This risk suggests that the initial delivery of 360 degree feedback reports should be considered very carefully... more on that later. The other thing that happens is that participants manage their upsets/disappointed emotions by a number of different strategies:

1. **Justification** – there is a reason worked up that explains it and justifies or excuses the results. They can be quite happy knowing the data is because of someone or something else being a certain way.

2. **Denial** – the very facts or experience are blocked and denied, there is an attempt to "forget". This shows up as losing the report, missing the coaching and/or ignoring or not really letting in the conversations.

3. **Minimising** – the importance or relevance of the data is minimised in an attempt to make it OK as "it doesn't matter" which covers up the truth about how much it really does matter.

4. **Resignation** – there is a feeling that there is nothing they can do, they are resigned to how it is. This is a tricky one as it can appear as if they are OK when really this mature sounding position may be a cover-up for a big upset.

5. **Giving up** – they throw their hats in! They may or may not declare that they are giving up but it is a common reaction to upset to consider it impossible, to think there is not any useful way forward, so give up. This also is difficult as it can appear like a level of acceptance and their real emotions may remain hidden.

6. **Projection** – rather sneakily the upset becomes focused on someone else, for instance the boss, the coach, or some other body, eg the 360 degree feedback project, the senior managers, etc. This blame deflects the emotions to others so it feels better but it belies the personal pain. This can be a real challenge as you are inevitably encouraged to defend and justify rather than talk about the real issue which is their data!

7. **Blame** – another level of projection is blame when a whole situation is blamed on a person or a thing. This is where they are clearly not taking responsibility for their own situation. Very tricky, especially when others may indeed have acted out of line and are to blame for some stuff. The integrity of your process is critical though to make sure there is nothing significant they can realistically "blame".

These responses are natural and normal and you are best being prepared for them. They are on the safe bank of "upset". The recommendation is to have a strategy to minimise the likelihood of such responses and also tactics to deal with them should they emerge. The key goal worth aiming for is to structure and support sufficiently that everyone gets to a position where they are able to take full responsibility for their data and their impact at work. And for them to be OK with having this responsibility (for past and future). A goal to empower your participants through the process works. Having people be "OK" is critical for development and learning that makes any real difference.

There are five stages to manage to minimise these coping strategies so they are OK:

1.   **Pre-engagement stage** – the very idea of 360 degree feedback can totally freak some people! Fear can kick in at the mere mention of it... There are those who are feeling insecure about their performance, who have a problematic relationship with their boss and do not feel comfortable at work and there are those who are highly sensitive to feedback of any kind, at any time.

The idea that you are just about to be given feedback has been compared with the experience of walking through a dark alley hearing footsteps approaching you from behind. It can be that scary a notion.

EXAMPLE

A respected member of my admin team had worked with us for 18 months and in a one-to-one, with some nervousness, she asked if she was going to have to do a 360, ever. *"Not specifically, why?"* got the desperate answer, *"I have been worrying about it for ages. Please don't make me do that!"* To settle the fear she was told that she would only participate in 360 degree feedback if she wanted to and my suggestion was, given that she had never done a 360 degree feedback before, that she first completed the survey on herself. It's one step at a time with some people!

More usually there is a range of anticipation, from extreme anxiety through to indifference and then to a real eagerness and hunger. In order to manage this stage you need to bear in mind the SCARF[62] needs (as described earlier in Chapter 2) and provide quality information, answering questions such as: *"When is it happening?"*, *"Why are we doing this?"*, *"Do we have to do this?"*, *"What happens to the data?"*, *"Who else sees my data?"*, *"What happens afterwards?"*. Positioning your communications with the intention of motivating and energising them to want to do this is useful.

2. **Engaging stage** – selling the 360 degree feedback to your participants is key throughout the active engagement stage. You want them to give their energy and time to choosing reviewers and to completing their own survey. They need to be reminded what is in it for them, why they are doing it and what goodies they will get once it is done. You may need to work on the PA/admin support of the more senior or busiest managers. Support them in making sure they have space in their diaries. Encourage them by booking the coaching/feedback session in their diaries at a mutually convenient time before the data gathering process even starts. Keep answering their questions, of course, as promptly as possible and with care.

3. **Seeing the data** – this is a critical moment. If your 360 degree feedback is designed well the participants will now be eager to see their data. They may think they will be happy being given it in a meeting or training course among their peers but they could

be so wrong! This is the danger zone. If there is an emotional reaction and the individual is in a public, social environment then they really have no choice but to expose their upset fully or to take on one of the coping strategies listed above – and neither is that helpful to you or to them! As a result of this, privacy and the participant feeling in control is key at this stage. Options are private distribution or emailing. None is failsafe, but if you are clear how you are planning to distribute the data then it can be up to them how they manage it, eg if a PA normally looks at their inbox they have an opportunity to give you a private email address. They need space and privacy to manage their initial reactions. They often benefit from a chance to talk with their friends or loved ones. They need time to gather themselves together for a mature coaching conversation. We recommend **48 hours before a planned feedback session**. Trial and error have lead us to this policy – enough time to process the immediate reaction, not enough time to dwell or get stuck. However the best laid plans can be scuppered as the coping mechanisms can kick in very early:

EXAMPLE

A highly ambitious 30-year-old guy in London media had some very tough data from everyone (apart from himself) and it was a total surprise. Despite every communication and briefing he did not spot the report in his inbox and had first sight while with an external coach in a glass-walled office with his own staff and reviewers in full view. It was horrific! After an hour of working it through with the coach, the emotional responses needed to be released and he was encouraged to go for an 'early lunch' and a long walk on his own. A few hours later he was able to talk further with the coach and then his boss and openly explore what could be done.

TIP: check participants have seen their data when you were expecting them to! The disorganised will not have looked, the arrogant will not have thought they needed to bother, those in denial will have "forgotten", etc.

4. **Cognitive processing of the 360 degree feedback data** – this is where the upsets and reactions get reviewed and when there is the opportunity to turn these new insights into real clarity and new committed actions. First you need to allow participants to see the data, to see it as it is and to let it in. There is a strong tendency for participants to only focus on the negative messages, such that the positive data almost disappears from view. The key technique that assists this "letting in" is **listening** along with encouraging them to speak about their reactions and current thoughts or feelings. Only then will they have space to process anything more. Dealing with their questions is also key – they will usually want to know the answer to the following questions: *"How good is this?"*, *"Why are my reviewers rating me differently?"*, *"Who is right?"*, *"How does my 360 compare with others?"* Then there is a heap of interpretation to work through where you are helping them get clear on what the data is really saying to them, what the reviewers' views are, why they may differ, what the consequences are for them and others and finally what they should therefore do about it.

The key process in reaching understanding is that of **generating hypotheses** whereby a theory about why reviewers are rating as they are is generated (if not a number of theories), and this is checked against the rest of the data (and other observations) to see if indeed it fits. A triangulation of data is the aim, ie three different pieces of data pointing to the same conclusion. This encourages a confidence and is a more robust position than simply referring to one, no matter the validity of the source. So the stages are:

- Helping them get present so useful processing can begin

- Dealing with questions/issues

- Clarifying the key messages, particularly the positive ones

- Generating explanatory hypotheses

- Checking hypotheses with other data

- Exploring possible consequences and impact, ie confirming meaning

- Being OK with all of this

- Pinning down priorities for focus

- Identifying possible actions for moving forward

5.   **Being back at work** – this can be so easy and magical if the participant has processed the data all the way through. If they are OK with their data and are up for further exploratory conversations with people, or instead are quite happy having been reassured things are totally fine, then they go back to their work with relief and get on with it. Even without effort they can end up behaving quite differently from before. However, if there is any degree of upset or emotion or disappointment then it can be a problem for people to engage back in role. They are expected to behave and perform just as before yet they now know about negative opinions they were ignorant of before so it can be awkward and even embarrassing or humiliating. Supporting them in this position is ideal, guiding them on how to handle it and on what to say. Sometimes you can mediate a tricky relationship through a post-360 conversation. This can be a key source of transformation.

> **TIP**
>
> Best to tell participants: *"If you are OK with your data then feel free to discuss and share your 360 degree feedback with anyone you choose, but if you are at all not OK then it means you are not ready and you should definitely get some more support or coaching first."*
>
> They are often relieved at this point!

Once the data has been processed there is this key step of "being OK with all of this". If the data is generally positive this may not be hard (although sometimes the data is so much more positive than fits the self-identity that this is not guaranteed), but if there are negative bits then this can feel impossible. Of course you do not like key others not being impressed, how could you!? There is no transformation unless there is an acceptance of this position though – instead there will simply be a sense of failure, disappointment, etc, which may then translate into resignation or depression depending on the coping strategies deployed.

Turning your 360 degree feedback data from "not OK" to "OK"

The first step is getting clear what the upset is really about, getting as specific as possible. *"Exactly what about this data do you not like?"* It may be one reviewer specifically, one particular behavioural rating, it may be one comment or it may indeed be the whole lot. Get that clear and you can start to unpick this and allow them to see where it comes from, encourage them to take responsibility for it and see how it is to be expected given their past, their role and their context and therefore how it is OK. And then they can start to see how it could be different or, alternatively, they see that it truly is perfect after all.

A common route of upset in 360 degree feedback data is an **unfulfilled expectation.** For whatever reason, you expect someone's opinion to be a certain way. That person may have said or done something to lead you to believe they had this opinion or judgment, or they may simply have omitted to say anything. They may have given positive appraisal ratings when the 360 degree feedback data indicates otherwise. They may have pretended they found your contributions at meetings helpful when they are now saying the opposite. They may have looked fine with you when they clearly never were. You might have had the experience of your team tending to like you and find you motivating but this one individual does not seem to. An expectation is not reality, it is only an expectation. It is, by definition, made up in your own brain. It may be entirely reasonable given the evidence to expect such things but it is nevertheless of your own creation. When you point out that underlying the upset is an expectation and was made up, then suddenly participants start to see it rather differently. You can exaggerate it rather and get them laughing as usually there is hilarity somewhere in the picture.

EXAMPLE

A high-potential software consultant in an American IT company was disappointed with her boss's ratings. They were OK but they were not as high as she expected and she was quite upset. I asked her what her expectations had been and she reported that she had had an appraisal just last week when they had said everything was totally fine and given her a high appraisal rating. I suggested that it was indeed quite reasonable to expect the 360 degree feedback ratings to be similar and then joked with her saying, *"Why on earth would you think the 360 would be the same? How ridiculous!"* We ended up wondering what could have happened and looking at various possibilities. The boss being over keen for her to have a big pay rise was one of the main options.

The other key access to being OK is clarifying the **meaning given**[63] to the upsetting data. Data is data is data. It is not intrinsically upsetting. You can look at many hundreds of 360 degree feedback reports and you can guess what will be upsetting to the recipients. Well, you can guess but you are likely to be wrong – this is not a logical or predictable phenomenon. Our cognitive processes are not necessarily sophisticated especially when the emotional centres are triggered so the meaning-making can go into overdrive quite easily. Check out what conclusions they are drawing. You might find that they are assuming that, now they know their peers do not fully respect them, it means they are no good and will have to leave. Challenge these decisions and conclusions. Even if you are suspicious that they may be right, it is not helpful for anyone to draw conclusions direct from data like this. Come right back to them with a *"How can you be so sure?"*, or clarify that it does not mean this at all, and describe exactly what the data is saying instead. Check other parts of the report and see if it is all backing up their conclusion – it may or may not be. The key thing to do is make sure they keep the doors open and their mind open to what it might mean. Usually the truly upsetting conclusions are only answered in proper dialogue in real life, not looking at a personal 360 degree feedback report.

There may be things the participant needs to **communicate** – either a need to express a frustration with someone, eg *"Why didn't you tell me in my appraisal that you weren't happy with my performance?"*, *"How dare you write these* *things about me, what are you playing at?"* Get these expressed in the safety of the coaching conversation rather than in real life. Then you can help them get clear how they are going to deal with it professionally and maturely.

There may be a strong sense that there is **something wrong** with their data and therefore with them and/or their work or life. They may wish to be better or different in some way. This can occur when there is an inclination towards perfectionism for instance and/or when there is a strong identity to want to be seen as "nice" and liked by others – when any lesser data challenges a deep-rooted survival requirement for these individuals. The coping strategies will be well rehearsed for these individuals and may well show up quite dramatically via torrents of tears or a passive aggressive projection on to the coach, so take good care not to trample into this territory without full permission and confidence. To usefully and carefully coach this aspect can be life-changing if you get it right but can be damaging otherwise.

Listening is the key skill to apply here as well as confirming what you feel and see. Try asking questions such as, *"Do you have any idea where this high expectation of yourself has come from?"* or stating, *"This idea of being liked has clearly worked very well for you up to now"*. Key is to highlight that, whatever they have been saying and doing, it has been for a very good reason and has been working for them. If it had not been working then, quite simply, they would have done things differently. This way you can allow them to get to be OK with how it has been and at the same time allow them to see that things might be different in the future.

They may take it all very **personally** and that might not allow them to see it in a mature way. They may be thinking and feeling that there is nothing they can do and feel quite helpless about this. This is not an empowering position for them to plan their actions. Here you can use a depersonalisation technique[64]. You can suggest that they could see themselves as an island surrounded by an ocean.

Depending on the weather, the time of year, etc, the sea comes in to the shore and the beaches are washed and the sand is worked, eroded and refined. The context you are working in is the ocean and the weather, ie the conditions you find yourself in. Your role, your boss, your company, the economy, the targets, your intention, your team, your health, your family all make a difference to how you show up and the 360 degree feedback data shows you what is happening at your shoreline, at the interface between you and other people.

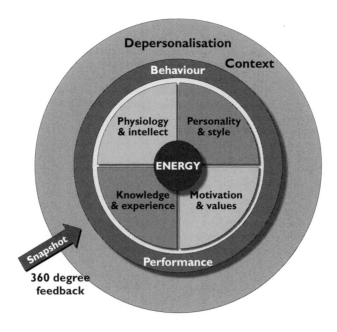

If you help your participant get clear on the specifics of their current context then they start to shift their perspective. Instead of seeing the data as being critical about them, they start to see it as a view of the relationships in the current conditions. Not just that, but a perfectly valid picture in these conditions. Once they see it this way they can see what can be done to change things. Shifting intention, tweaking job role, transferring priorities can be easy to do. Other changes may be harder to make but more attractive, eg change company, move country.

Making sure the reviewers are OK too

There can be an emotional ride for others in the 360 degree feedback process, not just the focus. The needs outlined in the SCARF model (see Chapter 2) apply equally to the focus's direct reports, their peers, their bosses and others less closely connected but who may be invited to participate. They all need to know what is happening, what the purpose is, what the real purpose is (they are likely to suspect more) and how their feedback and data will be handled. The whole process runs most smoothly if the focus is fully briefed and on board and they are instructed to invite and brief all their reviewers – that way the authentic personal request and true desire for their feedback is clearly communicated, and there is no doubt about this. However, back in the world of busy reality, this idea is a little idealistic. You may therefore need to plan in management team briefings, webinars for all reviewers, information packs, posters, video clips, Frequently Asked Question (FAQs) packs online, etc. You can access examples of such materials via the Talent Innovations website[65].

There are a number of insecurities, and training and information needs that need to be taken care of. There is the uncertainty about how exposed the data is going to be – the key question being: "*Will the focus be able to spot that it is me saying this?*" The answer to this of course depends on the construction of your survey and reporting parameters. And the truth is that, even with a lot of reviewers with only averages shown, it is possible that it will be clear that everyone has rated a few things really badly. If that is true and clear then, yes, it will also be clear that that individual rated that way too. Showing examples of the outputs to all reviewers is a clear and honest way of informing people and allowing them to decide for themselves what they want to write and rate, given what will be visible.

A line to take throughout this whole debate is to be clear that no one is wanting anyone to express anything they are not happy about the focus knowing. You could go even further – you might suggest reviewers should only express what they are willing to justify, should they be asked to.

It is easy to focus unduly on the issue of confidentiality of data as this is often a primary question or concern for reviewers. If you notice this happening, you might want to remind people that they should of course feel comfortable with the parameters of the project but that some company cultures (yes, even in the UK) would refuse point blank to give feedback confidentially. Some will only agree to give 360 degree feedback if their personal names are put to their specific comments and ratings. And they find it offensive to think they would be doing anything different. Maybe this is how most of us will be in years to come?

Reviewers need to be brought into the project in the engaging stage too and while their feedback is being requested. They might need to be encouraged, cajoled and thanked. They also need to be considered in the back-at-work stage once the 360 degree feedback data has been shared and processed by the focus. The ideal situation is that the focus returns to their reviewers and has conversations with each of them. This is specifically to thank them for their time and feedback but also to acknowledge some of the results and insights and potentially to enquire and explore it with them – to gain a deeper understanding of the true meaning of the data and to gain their support to move forward. Ideally the conversation will end up with a sense of sharing, a mature learning together and a clarity about what will be happening differently in the future. It helps the re-integration and re-wiring of the brain and installing of new habits if actions are defined in terms of how things are going to be in future. For instance, if the focus needs to work on preparing more for key meetings, then they could get clear with their team that: *"Whenever there is a client meeting in that week's diary then X will raise this at the weekly team review and steps will be agreed for adequate preparation"*.

The boss as a reviewer has all these needs but they often have additional issues regarding 360 degree feedback. Traditionally it was the boss's view that carried the day. In fact it probably was the case in the past that it was literally the only view that mattered – your job and your future totally depended on it. The boss could hire and fire, regardless of fairness, consistency, objective assessment, etc. Our employment rights and the legislation that supports them are fairly recent really – the first legislation trying to limit boss's actions appearing in 1875[66]. Professionals first emerged to support employee management post second world war[67] with the language of employee satisfaction starting to appear only in the 1990s[68] and now we are seeking the views of all sorts of people in trying to gauge how effective people are. Some managers will naturally feel threatened and a little confused about this. What about their power and the esteemed position of their views? Some struggle enough to own their authority as it is. So you need to be sure that this is fully taken care of.

In the pre-engagement stage those more senior need to be committed to the 360 degree feedback process and aligned to the objective. This is where things can go awry. They may think that gathering data on their people will be great, and once they see how useful and relevant it is they will want to see more, they will want to use it for recruitment decisions and to guide performance management and reward and more. The better the data, the more they will want it! So make sure you are very clear what the agreement is in terms of who sees what data and be careful to stick to this. Even if others are highly persuasive, do not change your mind.

The bosses have their own SCARF needs and status and control may be the key ones to satisfy. As well as being fully informed and briefed, consider being clear to give them a strong role in the process – whether it is to hold "development conversations" with their managers shortly after the 360 degree feedback sessions or whether it is to have a de-brief with the 360 degree feedback coach and be presented with a review of the aggregated data so they have special and full access to the team-level stats. In addition to this you can use the boss to refer to if there are issues emerging through the data-gathering process. You can also build in extra questions in the 360 especially for the boss and/or consult with them fully on the survey content so they are confident the most useful questions are being covered. Ensure it is their project as much as yours and you will maximise impact.

Logistics can be a challenge for bosses and they can benefit from careful managing and special attention. Anyone who has a lot of 360 degree feedback surveys to complete in one period needs some support. You can consult with them about timing, you can work with them or their PAs to ensure time is planned in their diaries for completion, you can print out the surveys so they can take them with them on a plane trip or you can have someone go through the questions on the phone if necessary. In addition to this you can set up measures to limit the number of surveys any one person has to do, eg the system can reject nominations if someone has already got six requests for feedback. An intention to take care of the burden on them will go a long way...

Providing support is critical

Not everyone completing 360 degree feedback will need or want support but it is hard to provide it after the event unless it is organised for everyone in the first place. Support can be compulsory or optional. It can be informal or formal and it can be provided by the trained or the untrained. Whatever you offer needs to fit within the context and purpose of your project and there are a few things to consider in setting this up.

Doing a 360 degree feedback can be a bit like going to the dentist. You know it can be really great, you know overall it is going to be "good for you" and you know that it may be quite painless. On the other hand you also know it could be pretty painful, if not totally traumatic. But either way, given a choice, you would prefer to go to a good dentist! The dentist does not change the starting point state of your teeth and gums but they are likely to make a big difference to the experience and potentially also the end result. The 360 degree feedback support is similar – it can make a huge difference to the experience and the end result for people, even though this fact may not be obvious to those who have had no issues with their personal 360 degree feedback (people with good strong teeth may not be so fussed), or who are emotionally very strong or totally lacking in sensitivity to others' views.

Setting up 360 degree feedback coaching sessions for everyone who participates is a good way to be sure those who need support get it automatically. It is also a useful way to be sure you know how it is going, what the issues are arising from 360 degree feedback, and it allows you to understand the whole data set. These sessions can be run by anyone trained in 360. Coaching skills are very useful but there are a number of skills that make a difference beyond the usual coaching requirements. A 360 degree feedback session is not simply coaching to the coachee's agenda – there is a job to do to help and guide participants through the whole pack of data and then you need to challenge interpretations and meanings as well as the unpicking of upsets or negative emotions. It is harder than a personality profile feedback as the data is harsher than a self-review style perspective. It is harder than a personal coaching session as it is not just the individual's agenda and perspective on the table. It is harder than a typical wellbeing counselling session as there is an immediacy in facing the data and there is a reintegration back to the role required. It is perhaps most akin to post-traumatic stress counselling and this requires very high-level skills.

You need a support that will guide overall interpretation. 360 degree feedback is a fine-tuned diagnostic instrument and if every little glitch is considered a problem then you can end up with a significant amount of over-diagnosis. This phenomenon has been observed in the world of medicine with the advent of new technology such as the MRI and ultrasound that can identify abnormalities that would otherwise have gone unnoticed. You might think this is good – surely you want to see all the abnormalities – but it is not so simple[69]. Abnormalities do not equate to "issues that need fixing" and seeing them all can lead to a strong sense of "something is wrong" which can undermine confidence if not resolved. It can lead to over treatment, eg surgery that is not essential. Spotting something is "off" does not mean it has to be fixed and it does not mean that it is the root cause. Another analogy to illustrate this is the sun's rays shining through your room. If the light is right you can see all the specks of dust and all sorts in the air but without the sun you cannot see them at all. They are always there and hoovering the air is not going to make much difference.

SUMMARY

360 degree feedback can elicit emotions and often does – before, during and after. For everyone, participants and reviewers alike. The trouble with this is that the emotions are usually not conducive for learning. Real development does not happen in moments of fear and upset. Learning does not take place when you are anxious or frustrated. Creativity has no place when you are worried. The trouble is that new, interesting data is what you are aiming for with 360 degree feedback and this is likely to generate emotions and yet you want development. This is the dilemma. To resolve this you need to be sure everyone gets the information and support they might need, whether they know they need it or not – just like booking them all in for the routine dental examination! This is the safe way.

C H A P T E R   6

How to feedback 360 for a state-shift result (1): The Discovery Method

"That's right, Five, always put the blame on others."

Lewis Carroll, *Alice in Wonderland*

EXAMPLE

When I left Heathrow for two years' work in the USA (Boston, MA), to others I was a "charming, bright, friendly, warm" person. How can I be so sure? My 360 degree feedback data of course. Fast forward to when I was back in the UK – when I walked back into SHL offices in Surrey I was *"loud, confident, brave and driven"*. I was of course the same person and had been largely delivering the same work as the previous two years (if not simpler, as the market was less advanced) but something had shifted beyond the norm. There were a number of state shifts actually, made easy by the security and safety of my environment combined with the subtly different cultural context I found myself in.

The clearest shift occurred on my way home from work one evening, having been in the US for three months. I had worked out by then that the local Bostonians I was working with thought I was *"aloof, detached and arrogant plus a big dose of authoritative"* – the opposite of nice. I could see that centuries of history helped form this opinion. My usual techniques were not working for me and I was struggling to get anyone to do anything for me or to feel anyone was on my side. It was horrid. I was lonely and frustrated. Nothing I tried seemed to work. I was seriously tempted to give up but my moment of insight when walking down Harvard Street from the transportation stop was to see that I had choice. I couldn't change their opinions but I could change how I felt about them so I dropped minding them disliking me. Such a relief! I walked in the next day and was a more relaxed version of myself and started being more self-expressed and having fun – what did I have to lose? I did not have any friends anyway! Within a few weeks the locals adored me and were literally asking me to stay another year. I do not mind if people don't like me now and find it gives me a great sense of freedom.

One small thought, insight, choice or decision and the whole world looks different. If the world looks different then your experience of life and work will likely be different. This is not an experience of "better" or "improved" or "fixed". This is not the stuff of development plans or identified weaknesses, this is the realm of paradigm shift and transformation.

The definition of paradigm shift is "a fundamental change in one's assumptions, approach or the way of thinking, driven by agents of change. It is transformational"[70]. This is a phenomenon of change that can be observed and experienced but, by definition, it cannot be controlled or forced. It is probably the case that the more you want someone to have a paradigm shift about themselves or their business, the less likely you are to get it. It is the individual having freedom to choose and control that allows them to turn in another direction. That in a nutshell is the HR dilemma. Unless this is understood the true value of HR is unlikely to ever be acknowledged.

What can you do to encourage paradigm shifts? There are four ways you can see them work. A shift in perspective will do the job and this can arise from a new view and from seeing fresh data or angles on current data. Second, intentions can be changed or altered. Someone aiming to "prove they can manage" can shift to aiming to "do a great job as part of a team" instead, and as a result their whole way of working will change direction and style.

Assumptions can also be questioned and challenged. You are operating the way you are based on the current assumptions you have right now. It is useful to remember that it all always makes sense. You can encourage a shift in assumptions by all manner of means – with new data, new opinions, new benchmarks, new experts or simply a new way of seeing the way it is. You may assume that life would be better if you stayed in this job but once you question that assumption you might discover that your life would be improved by a new role or company. A new assumption, a new way. Finally, the fourth easy way to shift states is to look at commitment. If you are committed to certain projects, certain people, certain results then you will be a certain way about them. You may find on reflection or through some new experience or information that you are committed to your wellbeing beyond these projects and in a moment you are clear that you need to give up your projects and retire! Paradigm shifts are simple – yet so hard when you are resisting. The pain that is experienced is the resistance. When you are not resisting, these choices get made easily and quickly. It takes a few seconds and it is done! 360 degree feedback can of course facilitate these shifts and the possibility is that every feedback session you manage leads to such shifts occurring every time. That would really be something, wouldn't it? This chapter describes the techniques and conditions to encourage this and, unsurprisingly, the key issue is how to minimise and avoid the resistance and then how to allow participants to see and hear new perspectives with sufficient support and safety for them to feel they can really see and feel this and then make their own choices. The quest is for clarity on the conditions for the flowing "river of transformation" to appear safe enough to enter.

There are four conditions for state-shift via 360 degree feedback:

- **Safety** – feeling comfortable enough to explore and shift

- **Insight** – new information, evidence, feedback, data

- **Understanding** – a sense of "getting" and understanding what is going on, of truly seeing reality a new way

- **Willingness** – a willingness to let go of the old view/way will only be there if there is something wanted or desired

Let us assume then that your participants are engaged in the 360 degree feedback process as they want something. The 360 is designed in line with your culture so it will be presenting data you can guarantee is seen as clearly relevant and important, if not inspiring, and your participant has had initial sight of it with privacy and sufficient briefing so as to know what is going on. They are now expecting to meet their 360 degree feedback coach for a two-hour feedback session and you have a precious one-time opportunity to make a difference. Let us look at how to structure this conversation and how to manage their emotions and inevitable resistance – labelled the '*360 Discovery Method*'.

The *360 Discovery Method*

Literally hundreds of two-hour 360 feedbacks were done before the six critical and sequential steps were clear. From this experience you can be clear that, if you work through these stages in the order described, the participant will get to be OK and you will have managed a transformational experience.

Beforehand however, you need to arrive, so let's look at the optimum conditions before you even start. There will be a specific time and place in the diary and a location will be booked. Even though you know you want two hours you may decide to only book the meeting for one or one and a half. (This is a trick one of my City investment bank clients gave me as she discovered her managers considered two hours as totally over the top and they were only committed to giving the process one hour. Her trick was to book the one-hour meetings two hours apart and most of them had no idea that they overran). It's all in the packaging. Aim for a private space such as a meeting room or someone's office, reasonably convenient for them but not too close to their work colleagues. Avoid meeting rooms that are too large or imposing and also those that have glass walls so that there really is no privacy. Hotel receptions and cafes can work if busy and anonymous enough but a meeting room is very much better.

Ideally you are sitting next to each other at a table for the 360 degree feedback report to be seen simultaneously by both of you. Coffee tables and comfy chairs do not work so well. You want to be the "right" distance from each other – this will differ depending on the culture and individual but check whether they look like they want to back away – don't keep pushing forward. Some participants may feel they want to start the meeting across a table from you. You can always start this way with an aim to move nearer and alongside as their comfort increases.

Make sure both of you are totally comfortable, swap business cards, ensure phones are off, a clock is visible to you (I tend to take my watch off and lay it on the table), that you have your notebook out and pen at the ready. You will have a nice colour-bound copy of their report there to present to them. They may have nothing or they may have brought a fully marked-up or highlighted copy of their report and they may have a notebook. Check you both have the drink you need and settle in gently, building rapport as you go.

Remember that there may well be a high level of anxiety about this session; they may have been dreading it for ages or only since they saw their data, but the *360 Discovery Method* is designed to allow you to manage and minimise the emotional load this automatically brings. Be relaxed and present yourself and work it through as described and it will be fine.

Each of the following stages will be described in full:

Structure for a 360 Discovery session			
STAGE 1	**Rapport**	Getting you both present, with credibility	5 min max
STAGE 2	**Boundaries**	Clarify objectives, boundaries and process	5 min max
STAGE 3	**Their goal**	Getting to know them and what they want	20 min max
STAGE 4	**Exploration**	Exploring the 360 data together	80 min max
STAGE 5	**Summary**	Summarising the position	3 min max
STAGE 6	**Commitment**	Over to them: their priorities and their commitment	8 min max

STAGE ONE
Getting you both present, with credibility
(5 minutes maximum)

It is easy to jump straight into the main conversation as both of you will be eager to do this but there is something you have to do first. It is a vital few minutes of introducing yourself and allowing them to download sufficiently for them then to be able to listen and engage fully. Start by introducing yourself with a short, succinct summary of who you are – perhaps your background, key facts about your career, be sure to make it clear that you are trained and experienced in 360 degree feedback (and other psychometrics?), that you have been coaching people at this level for X years and that you have been consulting or working in this industry/ company for X years. Specifically finish with a clear statement of what you are committed to in terms of this session.

> **EXAMPLE**
>
> My line is often: *"I am committed to working through this data with you so that you are really clear on the key points it is saying and so that you reach a conclusion on what your next steps will be. We may not understand it all and end up with more questions about it than answers but at least you will know how to progress. Is that OK with you? Great, let's start with you and your background..."*

At this point they usually relax visibly and you can see their confidence in the process growing. They are starting to trust me to handle their journey of exploration and it is clear that it is not a "me versus them" type of conversation – we are exploring this together.

Occasionally the participant is a real talker and it is hard to be sure I cover this point. Whenever I miss this though, I do not feel I have control over the session. If this happens, put your commitment in as soon as you notice – it is never too late. The critical words in that opening are *"I am committed"* or *"My commitment to you is..."* It gives a strong message, as you are saying you are not just there to listen to their views about their 360 degree feedback, you have a position and a commitment or promise that you are going to keep to. This is also vital when it comes to unpicking resistance later on in the session as you may be referring back to it. As you can see, each of these suggestions is there for a reason, miss them at your peril.

The other part to this stage is allowing the participant to express themselves and inviting them to share a key reaction, feeling or emotion about the 360 degree feedback process to date. You want to disguise this as an easy question – no heavy, deep and meaningful questioning yet...

> **EXAMPLE**
>
> *"Did you manage to read through your 360 degree feedback survey then?"* or *"How has the 360 process been for you so far?"*

The participant may respond in full or with not much but usually they will express something of where they are at. They may complain about the process, lack of briefing, errors with reporting, confusion about reviewers, frustration about their boss not completing. They may say they did not want to participate at all or that they were not sure it was going to be at all helpful. They may say some of the data is shocking or upsetting. They may say they are really confused about what it is saying or that they do not know what to do with it. Whatever they say, you listen and question further into specifics without getting embroiled. You apologise if there are any project, process or technical issues to apologise for.

If there are emotions at this point then acknowledge them without probing further. It is too early to deal with them but make sure the participant is left very clear that you have heard and that you want to look at what the data is saying in order to understand "where this is coming from" or "what might be behind these views". You may then want to state your commitment differently, eg *"We will look at this together and work out what you need to do moving forward"*. They may say very little, eg *"Yes, it is quite interesting, nothing that new, it's fine"*. Wherever they are up to, it is fine. And the key point is that, if there was a burning issue distracting them, they have had a chance to get it off their chest (and possibly resolved) and you now know where they are in terms of feeling and relating to their data.

Now they will be able to listen better and you are gaining a new level of rapport at the same time. The intimacy levels are getting closer but the participant is maintaining control while you are responding professionally and with empathy.

STAGE TWO
Clarify objectives, boundaries and process
(5 minutes maximum)

Once they are present, go straight in to describing the specifics they need to know to feel certain about the process. Describe the objectives of the 360 degree feedback and explain how it fits into the other related processes. Clarify the purpose of the session itself, explain who sees their data and what the plans are for follow-up. Deal with their responses and reactions to this information.

EXAMPLE

"So there is an intention to support the leaders of the business in this period of significant growth — to support you in 'stepping back and stepping up' and you are in the first cohort doing the Leadership Development Programme this year I gather? As you know the 360 degree feedback is the first stage of this programme and this has been designed specially to cover the leadership behaviours considered important for the future of the business. We are looking at this data so you can start to get clear how you are doing in these areas in your current role. The idea is that this will help you get really clear which areas you want to focus on through the programme — you will then know which are your priorities, and which aren't, and it will help guide the coaching that is running through the year too. Is that your understanding?"

"This 360 degree feedback data is yours. Only me, you and the confidential project management team at Talent Innovations see your report. We will be looking at the aggregated data of all of the senior leaders in due course and this data will be reported back to your group in the Development Programme in the first module so you will get a chance to look at the whole picture with your colleagues. This analysis will also be reported back to the HR team, the training team and the exec board as they are very interested in understanding better what this is saying about the current culture and what needs to be done to support you moving forward as a group. Is that OK with you?"

"Great, well we have until Xpm but don't worry about that, I will manage the time. I just want to reassure you that this session is totally confidential and between us. I will be feeding in general themes and observations but I will only share personal specifics with your permission. We can agree what is reported and what is not reported back at the end."

STAGE THREE
Getting to know them and what they want

(20 minutes maximum)

Once they are settled, clear and relaxed about the session you simply get them talking... you can start them at their first job, ask them to talk about where they were before this company, start with this job, whatever is appropriate for you.

EXAMPLE

"The objectives are to work through the 360 degree feedback survey with you but, given all this data represents what people have thought of you up to now in your current role and context, it would be really useful for me to understand your current situation fully.

"This data is already in the past and is only interesting really in terms of what it means for you in the future, so it would also be useful to understand what you are wanting in terms of your career, life, etc. Perhaps you can talk me through your career to date, clarify your current role, your challenges and frustrations and what you struggle with the most for instance. I would also love to hear your ambitions and thoughts about the future.

"To start, can you give me a short career summary of how you got to this job?"

Keep them moving if they talk a lot and get them talking if they are too succinct. The objective is for you to get to know them really well, to allow you to pick up clues about how they work, what motivates them, how they respond to failures and upsets, why they move between jobs, which activities light them up as they speak, which scenarios depress them. Take brief notes of key facts as they speak – it makes them feel important and you can later refer back to them clearly which can be very useful in working through the data. Look for trends and patterns. Feel free to make observations and to throw in some useful comments as long as you know they will support your objectives.

> **EXAMPLE**
>
> *"So, this was another situation when you got bored and moved on to another new challenge?"*
>
> and later it could be
>
> *"Thank you so much for talking me through your career — I can see that you started in this company as a very experienced accountant coming from a totally different sector and culture. That must have been quite a shock?" or*
>
> *"So, you really like managing creative teams — that is what you have loved doing?"*

Make mental or real notes of threads and motivations, values or critical factors that appear in the information. They will feel really well understood and ready for the more rigorous critique the data leads you to.

Make sure you are really clear on the current role and how they feel about this job and its challenges, whether they enjoy it, how well they are doing, how long they have been in the role and how well it suits them. This may take some further questioning on your part:

> **EXAMPLE**
>
> *"What are things about this job you like the most?" and*
>
> *"What are your biggest challenges right now?"*

The second and critical part of this stage is to complete this career exploration, being really clear on where they are going. This may emerge naturally but usually needs to be asked specifically with a follow-up question:

> **EXAMPLE**
>
> *"So, where next then?"*
>
> *"What are your career ambitions now?" or*
>
> *"What would you like to be doing in, say, three years' time?"*

For those who are ambitious and clear about their next goal this will be all you need to extract the information, although you may need to question the specifics to get very clear. Aim to find one goal or thing they want in their career/life. Be aware of the general reluctance to spill the beans on these goals – the British culture does not make ambitions that easy to work with. Clarifying the specifics may sound like this:

> ### EXAMPLE
>
> *"So, you will be looking for the next step – what would you ideally like your next job to be?"*
>
> or
>
> *"By when do you want to be MD?"*

You are aiming for a very specific goal – a job or project or position and a very specific time. It could be a new challenge, a new job, a new boss or extra responsibility, an easier relationship with the boss, an outstanding appraisal rating, a great result for a project, a pay rise. It really does not matter what it is as long as they really want it.

Take care to specifically write down this goal in full – with all the detail they give you and the timeline. If they do not give you a timeline then question until you are clear to a reasonable level:

> ### EXAMPLE
>
> *"So, how would you feel if you haven't got this promotion by the end of this year?"*
>
> *"By the end of next year?"*
>
> *"In three years?"*
>
> *"OK, so you would really like a promotion by 20XX at the latest?"*

For some there is a definite disinclination to clarify a goal. My estimate is that over 70% of participants who hesitate to pinpoint what they want are women which fits the norm often stated. It appears to be the case that it is not as acceptable or desirable for a woman to be driven and ambitious and this may serve to discourage women from getting their goals clear.

With those who are timid at stating their desires you need to work harder. Question and then, if that fails, make suggestions. Make the assumption that everyone does indeed want something and it is your job to work out what this is. It is critical that you do this because, if you are not positioning the 360 degree feedback data inside something they want, you will simply be dwelling in the mass of opinion without direction which makes it very easy for people to be upset and stay upset. To be sure you can take care of them you need the hook of what they want.

Here are a few more ways to get this clear:

> **EXAMPLE**
>
> *"Well, would you like a new challenge or a new job at any point?"*
>
> *"How about a promotion?"*
>
> or you can try other angles:
>
> *"Are you wanting further qualifications or training at all? A different boss? Would you ever leave this company? Would you like an easier work–life balance? How about an improved relationship with your team? Would you like to be more confident as a leader?"*

The hardest participants to work with at this point are those who have given up and/or are near to retirement. The toughest one I remember was on a management development programme for "something interesting to do" and was due to retire in six months. After some desperate questioning and attempting the *"What legacy would you like to leave?"* angle, we got clear that she wanted an easier time with her boss for the rest of her time there. Phew! That I could work with.

This may be the first time they have got clear on a goal in this way, so this target is worth acknowledging and you may want to explain that you cannot guarantee they are going to manage this but affirm that the conversation is all about helping them get there:

> **EXAMPLE**
>
> *"Great, well let's see what your 360 degree feedback report is telling us about how you can achieve that."*

Give this stage all the time you need to get fully connected and have a clear specific they want. Whenever I have given up and moved on without this I have totally regretted it. You can go back and return to the question once you are into the data but this is tough to do, hence why it is worth bottoming out now.

Now, finally, you can move to the report.

STAGE FOUR
Exploring the 360 degree feedback data together
(80 minutes maximum)

First you start by announcing that you are moving into the data by describing how you are going to go about this:

> **EXAMPLE**
>
> *"Well this is your report – let's work it through together."*

You may want to adjust your seating and table so you are both looking at the report at the same time. It is time to get a little closer...

First you need to cover the detail of the first page if you haven't already. Ask them about their reviewers:

> **EXAMPLE**
>
> *"So, why did you pick these people to give you feedback?"* or
>
> *"Tell me about these reviewers?"*

Asking their reviewers' names is a great way of covering them fairly succinctly as it gives you their names and some key data about them (how long they have worked for them and what sort of relationship it is, are the most useful aspects to look for). Note the names down in your pad as you may want to refer to them later. It is much more powerful later to ask, *"What opportunities does, say, Peter, have to see you do this?"* than to ask them *"What do your colleagues see of this?"*

Cover the introduction pages and any explanation of the process or the competency framework. It is useful to position the instrument as based on those behaviours considered to be important to the future of the organisation, and to add that how these behaviours prioritise and play out will differ for different roles and to indicate that this is up to them to work out. This gives them the space to make their own decisions about what is going to be important rather than inviting them to justify why some of the questions are not as relevant as others. Take every opportunity to avoid resistance!

Now you turn to the data. (The next chapter deals with the specifics of interpreting 360 degree feedback data so for now this deals with process points rather than content.) For the first pages of data you need to guide them and inform them about what it is saying. Your job is to summarise the overview and the key points but very quickly to move on to asking them what they think about it. The main objective is to get them talking about what they are taking from the information. This way you can tell if they are interpreting it accurately and you can be in dialogue about what this is saying about them. As a general point, you will need to explain and interpret the more sophisticated charts. With these the emphasis is on checking with them what they are taking from it. Other charts, especially when you have got into the flow, may be easy to understand, so rather than you summarising or explaining, it is about giving them time to review and then checking their interpretation once again and helping them explore links with other parts of the data. The aim throughout is to assist the participant to get clear what the data is truly indicating.

> ### EXAMPLE
> *"This page shows an overview of how all your reviewers as a group rated you on each of the competencies – you can see that they rate X the highest and Y at the low end. Overall these average ratings are all above 3.8 and as 3 is rated satisfactory and 4 is good, this is a good solid set of ratings."*

Watch every word that you use. Describe the charts with 100% accuracy and without meaning that you cannot justify. Then you can enter the world of meaning but be led by them. Ask them what they think about this:

> **EXAMPLE**
>
> *"What do you think about this?"* or
>
> *"Does this surprise you?"* or
>
> *"How are you about this?"*

Get their response and deal with it if you need to, but at this stage put your energy into listening to their responses rather than making sense of what they are saying. Acknowledging their reactions is very useful. If there are dramatic responses at this stage you are best putting them into a "holding" position with these – making sure they know you will deal with this but asking them to do so only when armed with more of the data.

> **EXAMPLE**
>
> *"So you're quite disappointed with this. What specifically are you disappointed with?"*
>
> *"I can see you're really pleased with this. What were you expecting?"* or
>
> *"What is it you are not happy about?"* or
>
> *"So you expected the people-oriented competencies to come out higher? OK, well let's see as we go through the report what is going on here."*

Your general aim is to listen very hard and to acknowledge their responses with full respect and as if nothing is wrong. Bring curiosity and puzzlement as well as calm peacefulness. Then participants will have room to be emotional and you will be in the best position to make a difference. You are not going to reach clear or well-informed conclusions looking at the early pages of data, yet they are likely to want to do exactly that. Your job is to encourage them to hold their decision-making, to allow them to see all the data before making firm conclusions and even to encourage them to delay concluding until they have had post-360 conversations with their reviewers. With decisive, action-oriented, wanting-to-fix-things-as-quickly-as-possible-types this is quite a challenge!

You move through the early pages in this way and you may find you are starting to form an interesting picture. But each page should give you some new perspective to cover, a new angle, some new detail. You need to make sure that the conversation is an easy mix of you talking them through a chart or piece of data combined with them talking you through how they are looking at it. The process at first is one of interpreting and questioning what is behind the data which then leads to hypothesis generation[71]. As you progress through the data, it becomes more of a dialogue where you are challenging, offering ideas, suggesting different hypotheses, pointing out connections and links, giving suggestions as to what might be going on at the same time as they are sharing their thoughts and insights. It is dancing in conversation all the way through this section and time passes very quickly!

EXAMPLE

"This looks like you are seen as very dynamic and driven by all your reviewers. What do you think about this?"

"Others see you quite differently in terms of vision and strategy – might that be linked to your communication style?"

"Your boss sees you very differently across the board – what do you think is going on there?"

"What do you make of this page?"

"Anything new here for you?"

It is difficult to be prescriptive given this dance and team approach to interpretation but there are some critical moments to manage – one of them is the pages of open free text.

What other comments/feedback do you wish to provide in order to assist John in his role?

"I think John is very good at the specific role on an account-by-account basis but I think he could improve by carrying a dynamic general role across the claims business – giving understanding to the wider picture of the market and taking a pragmatic view of the challenges and opportunities."

"To carry on encouraging the team and helping with the development of others within the team. To continue to work hard and contribute to develop new skills."

"John is an open, approachable and friendly character who is always a pleasure to work with. He has built a strong and trusting relationship with the reserving team and we are appreciative of the expertise and insight he provides.

"I would ask that John continues to keep in mind our layman understanding of claims-related matters. Some of the terminology and finer points will be beyond us, and on occasion it's difficult for us to cut through the extensive amount of detail John may present in order for us to determine the high-level overview and recommendations (from John) we are looking for. This is often exacerbated by the tight timescales my team are required to work to. I appreciate though that striking the right balance between the level of detail appropriate is claim dependent and we are happy to continue to work with John in the collaborative way, already established, to achieve that balance.

"In the transition between claims team heads, John has noticeably stepped up to help fill the resource gap, and to thereby help ensure that the standard and level of support that the reserving team require from claims colleagues was maintained. On behalf of my team I would like to thank John for all his hard work and we look forward to our continued productive working relationship."

"While John's strengths are his attention to detail, his routing and his set manner, a development area is for him to become more creative and to add more flare to his work. Added to this he should work at change management – this will all lead to improved contribution to the business as well as his personal development."

"John should be looking to develop his skillset. He tends to rely on being told where he needs to develop. He usually identifies areas for development though may not conclude."

What do you think he is particularly good at in terms of displaying our Values and Core Behaviours?

"Accuracy and attention to detail."

"I think John is strong across all the company values. With respect to our core behaviours, John is very accurate and attends to detail but sometimes needs to infer what information the placing team is fundamentally concerned with and what the key requirements are."

"Mainly the teamwork aspect of the values we encourage, along with achieving excellence through hard work."

"John is incredibly focused on detail, service and his contribution to his team, peers and the business."

"John is a very strong people person and quickly and efficiently builds relationships. He is trustworthy, very committed and reliable."

"Attention to detail, approachable, good at praising others."

Some participants will already have highlighted some statements within the pages of open-text feedback, others may not even have read it all yet. Either way, your job is to have them re-read it all with their newly informed mindset and your support. There are a couple of ways to achieve this:

EXAMPLE

"What did you think about your open feedback?"

"Any surprises in there?"

"Which bit pleased you the most?"

"Which comment did you like the least?" or

"Why don't you re-read this in the light of what we have been talking about?" or

"Why don't I go to the Ladies and leave you to read this through in peace?"

If you feel the participant needs some privacy and space to properly take in their data (regardless of the open text) this is a great excuse to leave them. Often magical processing has happened in my absence so don't be surprised at what might happen. The main thing you are looking for, however, is the bits that have upset them in some way. Your main job is to encourage them to speak up and let you know what has disappointed or angered them. Bear in mind that most people will be very determined not to let on to anyone that there is a piece of data or feedback that has left them feeling humiliated. Talking about it is even more humiliating. But if you know there is a reaction you can help them handle it and feel more comfortable. You may have to show guile though...

Throughout this stage of the session you may think you will be able to tell what is likely to upset people and what will be fine. This is a trap. You have no idea. Innocuous-looking data can leave one person devastated with shame and horribly harsh-looking data can be accepted with grace and ease and with full expectation. There are some tips which indicate potential for upset however – when self-ratings show they are highly sensitive to feedback (and others have no clue) and when self-ratings are significantly more positive than important others' (the boss's opinions often, but not always, being the most crucial). Be on guard in these situations.

This stage ends when you have looked at every page of the 360 degree feedback report. This may take some driving and speeding if there is full debate and discussion early on, but if you have covered important ground already then usually the latter pages simply add a little more colour to your initial conclusions rather than add new evidence. If you have prepared, you will know whether you need to save time for new nuggets of course. To move quickly yet respectfully through data, here are a few tips:

> ### EXAMPLE
>
> *"Anything new here for you?"*
>
> *"Anything else here you want to discuss?"*
>
> *"Anything here that concerns you?"*

Finally you have covered all the pages and looked at all the data with the participants. Every concern has been discussed, every low rating has been reviewed, every highlight has been acknowledged, a range of hypotheses and themes have been discussed and you are satisfied that nothing has been left un-discussed that should be. There may have been reactions and disappointments emerge through this discussion and you should have been able to assist in these (more on these techniques later). They should feel OK and relieved you have completed the job of full review. You should have been monitoring the time throughout and you will be aiming to turn the last page no later than 10 minutes before your finish time. Prioritising the most critical pieces of feedback is important, otherwise these sessions can go way past the two hours.

STAGE FIVE
Summarising the position
(3 minutes maximum)

Visibly indicate the end of the data review by closing the report, picking it up and handing it over to them (with a bit of ceremony if you can manage it).

> ### EXAMPLE
> *"Well, we have gone through everything in your 360 degree feedback report so here is your copy to keep."*

Sit back, pick up your notebook and take on a different energy. You may even want to adjust your seating to be a bit more formal or distant, as this is a different conversation. You start by volunteering a summary and acknowledgment of what you have seen through the data and the conversation. This needs to come from your heart, not just to be a repeat of the data but your own take on it. Aim to be empowering and constructive in your summarising.

This is your opportunity to give the broadest, biggest picture of what is going on for this person. You can provide a positive, big context for them to see their data. Just a few sentences that usefully summarise:

EXAMPLE

Overall good data:

"Perhaps I can summarise what I can see in your data. You are highly respected and valued in this role. Your reviewers totally appreciate your thinking and your ideas, as well as how you manage relationships. It looks like they may be wanting a little more direction and structure in some areas but, as we have discussed, you need to get clear exactly what is needed here. You are totally committed to doing a great job which is clearly inspiring – you can see this in the data and I can see it too. Thank you for such a constructive discussion! How are you about your report now?" or

Mixed data:

"Let me summarise by saying that I can see you have really been struggling in this job. It is a totally different culture compared with what you are used to and your boss and your team seem to be quite unsure how to manage you. You don't really know how best to manage them either! You have been aiming to fit in and be positive but this strategy seems to have led others to be a little suspicious of your motives. As we have discussed, it may be time to review your intention – re-focusing on your big initiative of bringing innovation to the company instead of working to be liked across the organisation may be more effective. What do you think?" or

Poor data:

"Perhaps I may summarise by saying that, despite your best efforts over the last year, others do not seem to be appreciating you as leader. They see you as a strong expert but they do not see where you are trying to take them. Your leadership brand seems to be strong, dynamic, vocal and confident expert. I am not sure how well this fits with your ambition to be promoted to director level – what do you think?"

This is not news as you have already covered all the data, but the summary should serve to make the overall position really clear – not that there is anything wrong, not that you are pretending it is better than it is, but you are happily giving them the final mirror of transformation. Make sure you position this as your view and your perspective – it is not the truth and it is up to them how they take it and what conclusions they draw. Maintaining this attitude will minimise potential resistance.

Now you give it over to them...

STAGE SIX
Over to them: their priorities and their commitment
(8 minutes maximum)

You have heard their general feeling and response to their 360 degree feedback and they have expressed themselves as much as they wish on the matter. Now it is time to pin them down:

EXAMPLE

"So, if you had to choose three areas to focus on moving forward, what would you pick?" or

"So, what are your priorities in progressing this?"

This is the time to wait with your pen in hand. You need to leave space for them to think and decide for themselves. Their processing can feel like a long time to you, but it will not feel a long time to them so just relax. It is wonderfully surprising what then emerges. They may not focus where you think they should, there may be a new area that was not obvious in the data, but this is them and their career so just delight in what they see as priority. Take notes of what they say and question it to get it clear and specific. In this session it is about exploration and understanding, not detailed development planning, so you will likely only get as far as headings for areas. This was your aim and you should be satisfied with this. You can help them by clarifying what their next actions are and reminding them what is to follow. A follow-up coaching session, a training module, or a career development meeting with the boss will all serve to encourage and motivate the forwarding actions.

You can end by summarising the priorities for focus:

EXAMPLE

"That's great – you want to review the way you communicate with your team, discuss how to improve your strategic thinking with your boss, and look at how to get more feedback and training in giving formal presentations. You can brief your coach on where you have got to on this."

Then you complete the session with a thank you and a clarity on their next steps:

> **EXAMPLE**
>
> *"Brilliant, that's great. I think you will find the Leadership Development Programme and coaching really useful to support you in these areas. You may want to make a note of these actions in your module development planner. I really want to thank you for being so open and willing to explore things.*
>
> *"I have really enjoyed it and hope you have found it useful. I would really appreciate it if you would complete my review form to give me feedback on how this has gone for you – do you want me to leave you for a few minutes while you fill it in?"*

If they hesitate then of course you can leave it with them to return later, or you can ask them to return it to someone else. You need to protect their privacy all the way through to the end of the process!

SUMMARY

This is the two-hour *360 **Discovery Method***. The recommendation is to follow this process in all cases. It is designed to minimise resistance and to allow the participant to take full ownership of their data with maximum contribution from you in terms of insight and interpretation, so... it works! However, even if you do follow this, participants will react and respond emotionally – you can guarantee this. You just cannot guarantee exactly where, how and when! So, there is another process that you need to follow in parallel to keep them in the river of transformation instead of on the "bank of resistance". If you manage to follow both processes simultaneously and if you manage to maintain your calm and presence of mind fully, you can pretty well guarantee a state shift will occur – as long as there is useful new data of course...

C H A P T E R   7

How to feedback 360 for a state-shift result (2): The four levels to managing resistance

"Living for others is such a relief from the impossible task of trying to satisfy oneself."

Alain de Botton, Philosopher

The six steps of the *360 Discovery Method* (as described in Chapter 6), in the right order, will take you and your participant through a transformational conversation. However, there is another separate process to take with you on this journey and this is the management of resistance.

Participants will turn up open and truly ready to be coached and explore their data, or they won't. They may start OK but react defensively to a low rating or a bit of open-text feedback. The transformation opportunity you have will not amount to much if they stay this way. Their hormones and brain habits will ensure that they only hear a bit of what you are saying and only see a bit of what the data is really saying. It will be OK, they will make sure they survive the session however they do this, but you may want more for them than this.

This chapter describes in detail how to deal with this "resistance" and unhelpful emotional responses. Again there is an order to this, but instead of a straightforward sequential process such as the *360 Discovery Method*, ie first you do this, then you do this and then you do the other, this is an order of seriousness or level of intervention, ie first try this, try this a few times – if that does not work then try the next level, if that does not produce results then go up a level, etc. If someone is extremely resistant you may go through these levels very fast and reach the highest level within an hour. Most people are likely to require level one and two interventions only, repeatedly and mixed up as you go through, and you never need to reach level four. Only the hardcore few get this far.

Let's start with level one – the common coaching position of exploration – the level you hope you may never have to leave:

LEVEL ONE: Listening, making safe and deep questioning

Acute, deep listening makes a difference[72]. This is where you reflect back what you are hearing and feeling. You summarise what has been said. You bring things already said earlier in the session into a particular conversation. Listen with all your power and all your body. The participant may be saying, *"That's OK, I can see where that data has come from"* but you may feel a deep sadness, and on reflection you can hear there is a sadness and sense of resignation being expressed. How you respond to this will depend on your own training and confidence, but your own acknowledgment will make a difference even if you do nothing obvious at this stage except give them the space to feel this.

This is a place for acknowledgment, confirming your own experience of them, questioning what you see and hear. You need to be fully present and OK while this is going on so that this will be what you give them – a sense that it is OK to feel and think whatever they are experiencing.

EXAMPLE

In a Scottish aeronautic manufacturer a senior manager was looking at his 360 degree feedback for the first time (this was before I worked out I needed to send the 360 report 48 hours before) and was not happy. He started a little anxiously and as he worked through the data he became frustrated, then, rather rapidly, very angry. He was gone. He was not hearing any of my questions or comments aiming to calm him. I was tense and at quite a loss – anxious myself.

I then took space and deliberately calmed my breathing. I unlocked my legs (which I had discovered were tightly wound round each other like only long skinny legs can be), lowered my shoulders and lent forward a little. Within minutes I noticed he started to do exactly the same. He relaxed, started breathing and calmed. After what felt like a long time (maybe only a few minutes), he spoke. I can't remember what it was but I am pretty sure it was rude. I responded with a gentle clear *"Yes"* and soon he turned back to me and we talked properly again.

This extreme example shows the power you have as a committed listener and reflector. It may seem like you are just a passive mirror but any mirror has an action and a potential reaction. You can also be a very active mirror. There are some fundamental principles underlying this approach – first there is the belief in the power of reflection[73] and there is also the principle of individuals responding in a social context[74] combined with the transformational principle of giving choice and freedom to individuals[75], allowing them to be and to feel as they do and supporting them in choosing how to move forward.

You do not need to worry about these principles too much but, at this level, you do need to concentrate on being present and to focus on your questions and your statements very carefully. Your primary job at this level though is to make it safe for them, so let's cover this and then explore what you need to do and say in more detail.

Making it safe

Your participant will only be able to move forward if they feel safe and comfortable. As per the SCARF needs highlighted through neuroscience (see Chapter 2), if they are feeling as if their status is undermined, things are not fair, etc, then they will be led by their unconscious primal functions. So first you need to bring them back into the world of safety and conscious intellect. There is no one way to do this, but the key technique is to discover or guess what their main concern is and to handle this. If you focus on their privacy and control then this will usually resolve most of these needs, whatever the leading ones are:

> **EXAMPLE**
>
> A senior executive in a City firm was looking at his 360 degree feedback for the first time (in this case because he had not found it in his inbox and had been confident enough not to be bothered). His data was shockingly bad – even to him. He reacted with a tense silence and said how mortified he was. I pointed out that this data was his and no one else in the company had had sight of it and that it was now up to him what he did and who he showed it to. He relaxed and we could then continue to talk sensibly about what had happened and what his options were. Fear of loss of face was clearly primary for him and once he knew he had control, he took control.

If you struggle to make it safe for them, then ask specifically what would make it comfortable for them to discuss this, ask them directly what they are most worried about. There is another principle at play here which is to deal with the uppermost issue[76], the one that is currently on the surface and exposed. You may think they really ought to deal with their arrogance as it is clearly the big issue, but if they are bothered about their team not liking them then actually that is what is to be dealt with.

How do you know you have managed to ensure they feel safe? They will be relaxed and they will be giving you eye contact and they will be present.

Deep questions

Once they feel safe you can question and encourage them to explore[77]. Here are some of the most powerful questions you can use at this level:

1.   What do you think is going on here?

2.   Why do you think he/she/they have this view?

3.   What do they see of this?

4.   Why might their views differ?

5.   Who is likely to be the best judge of this?

6.   What are the reviewers trying to tell you do you think?

7.   What do you see as the main message here?

8.   How might this data link to earlier data? Might there be a connection?

9.   How do you feel about this data?

10. What conclusions do you draw from this data?

Notice that you are inviting them to consider and that you do not know. The critical piece you can offer your participants is a curiosity and an unknowingness. That will invite them to truly explore and be curious themselves. You are positioning them as the master of their own data yet you are challenging them. If you are someone who needs to "know" and have certainty about things then this may take some doing. You need to let go that you know what the data is saying and then paradoxically, you and your participant will emerge knowing eventually.

You are aiming to have them stop and think, to see the data properly and fully and to consider and feel the impact. This is the river of transformation. So, listening and questioning may be all you need to do to have them really "get" their data but you may need to go to level two.

LEVEL TWO: Feeling the impact

Let's assume there is something interesting in the 360 degree feedback report and you do not feel they are truly appreciating the significance of this, even after your best attempt at exploring and questioning. This level is about encouraging them to consider and feel the true impact and potential consequences.

Why is this such a good idea? Well, in my observations, it is a key step in transformational processes. There is a very basic premise that assumes that people do things for good reasons. Everything anyone does, they do it for what seems like a good reason to them. Others may consider them totally daft of course, and you can have a situation where literally everyone around you thinks something different from you, so even if others think you should do something differently you will have good reason not to. If you did not have good reason then of course you would do things differently. There is a logic in the way people work. If you truly get into the logic you can attempt to unpick it, but people are very well tuned to preventing anyone in to mess with their logic. They like their stories about themselves, they are deeply vested in keeping them as they are as their whole lives are built on top of them – why on earth should they change them? So, they need to see that there is sufficient at stake, there is a significant impact that is worth a re-evaluation. And anyway, who is anyone else to say that they should indeed change their views and thoughts about themselves – it is their call. So, key to this stage of managing resistance is your being firmly and clearly in a position where it is totally OK for them to be where they are. Then they will feel they have choice.

So you need to bring two things to this level – a clarity and exploration of what is at stake and what the consequences might be, and a freedom to choose options and stay as they are (and then they will feel they can choose a new way too). This latter point can be quite scary and difficult to accept for many consultants and HR people – the clearer you are about how bad this current situation is for them, the harder it can be to grant them the option not to change. Be brave, have a go with this approach – let go that you have any right or permission to have opinions about how other people manage their lives and all sorts may emerge – you may be surprised at how easy this is and how useful it can be!

EXAMPLE

The CEO of a City investment bank was "testing out" the 360 degree feedback process as he wanted everyone else to do it. His data was strong and good across the model with highlights in dynamism, specialist expertise and dealing with complexity, but it did have some low ratings in the area of listening and openness to others' ideas. There were also low-ish ratings from his direct reports in terms of motivation and engagement. We explored the data fast and he seemed to understand it well and openly. He could even see the possibility of a link between these two low areas but his response was, *"Well, that's my style. If they can't keep up I need to move on and don't have the time to work any other way."*

Time to engage level two so I asked him, *"What is the impact of this style (using his terminology) on your ability to drive a supremely successful business (the previously agreed goal)?"* The response was more considered – he thought and eventually said, *"Well, I guess it's not great is it? But what can I do about it?"* and then followed a full exploration of what was behind this "style", what the crucial moments really were for his people and what alternative strategies he could realistically deploy. He ended up clearly wanting to test out a few ideas with his PA to see what she thought which resulted in him holding Friday lunchtime sandwich sessions which gave everyone in the office a chance to talk with him and the other senior leaders. Result!

"What is the impact of X on your goal of Y?" This is a terrifically simple question that can change everything. You can see that you cannot even ask it if you have not got a clear, agreed goal to refer to though – hence why that stage in the **Discovery** process is critical. If ever I don't have a goal to refer to (very rare these days) I find myself totally floundering at this stage and just get more determined to pin down that thing that they want.

Sometimes the participant does not see the impact on their goal in anything other than an *"It's OK"* type of light. This may be because it genuinely had been OK up to now. In fact this is a key aspect of reality that is worth acknowledging as it is true – the 360 degree feedback automatically refers to the past (opinions from before now) and, given they are actually alive and employed right now, it must have been OK. So it really does take an openness of mind to be willing to see that maybe it is not OK for the future. They need to be reassured that things can be different as this will stop them relating to it as not OK.

One question on impact may be sufficient, but sometimes that doesn't quite work and you need to work a little harder in this level of intervention. Here is an example of a tougher one:

EXAMPLE

The FD of a telecommunications company in the home counties was doing a 360 degree feedback alongside his board-level colleagues (just to encourage them?) and his data had significant low ratings relating to listening and managing conflict constructively. This was coming from colleagues and reports, less from his boss with whom he had a positive relationship (although he thought the CEO was too soft).

Level one meant he understood the data and he was actually quite amused by it. If anything this was encouraging him to think less of his colleagues, "*Well, they are weaker than I thought – they shouldn't be shy in coming forward with their views!*" I asked the level two question, "*How does this impact your chances for promotion to group FD do you think?*" and he was clear it made no difference.

I then asked the secondary level question, "*How does it leave your colleagues then?*" This stopped him and he thought about it and eventually came back with, "*I don't know*". I was then able to point him to the report where there was feedback on exactly this issue which was that his colleagues were asking him to intervene and guide them more proactively. I then connected this feedback to the potential impact on the business and his ability to be an inspiring leader as a group FD. Then we could discuss what could be done.

Getting to "*I don't know*" is a good result in this level – in any level. A position of curiosity and not knowing is a healthy one both for you and them. You can then add in hypotheses which is a useful way of moving towards an opinion or judgment without being too definitive. You can then look for more data and information to see if these hypotheses fit. As an aside, this is a useful technique to use if your participant has interpreted data in a particular way which you think might be wrong – see the following example:

EXAMPLE

"They are saying this about my listening because we had a big row about cutting costs the other day." You think, *"Hmm, not sure about that"* and you say, *"Well that is one hypothesis to explain it. Are there any others? I can see one you might want to consider."*

After waiting for their reflection you might then offer yours, *"Any chance it could be because you do not rate your direct reports' views particularly and that could leave them feeling like you aren't interested in listening?"* If he does not see this then you can still leave this second hypothesis on the table for checking back to later, *"Well, let's see if there is any data later on which will confirm either of these – you may even have to ask them directly to find out the real answer."*

This level takes just one carefully selected question or a few choice questions, and as you can see it can take your participant to a whole new perspective on their data and their future. You can always tell that this is working from their reflection or a change in how they are holding themselves. They may sit back, or come forward. They may cry. They may look a little wet-eyed. The point is that the shift only happens if they feel the impact. If they simply talk about it in the same manner as they have previously been talking then they may only be seeing it intellectually. You may need to make it safer and more reassuring for them to allow them to get it emotionally. This is where the transformation occurs and these emotional reactions may then need to be supported and managed carefully... more about that later.

Even though this stage has a good success rate and generally does work, it is not guaranteed as resistance can kick in to prevent people seeing and feeling the consequences, but do not worry, there are further stages at your disposal:

LEVEL THREE: Sharing the impact on you

Hopefully you will not need to use this too often as it is very powerful but not for the faint-hearted. I would estimate that about 5% of my 360 degree feedback sessions reach this level.

They understand the data and you have explored the potential consequences for them, their goals and for others. You have tried all you can to get them to see how this really is for them and you think there is something here they are not seeing. You can tell they are resistant as either they are making this extremely obvious via body language, or from what they are saying about the process or because they are continuing to "talk about" their 360 degree feedback data in the same knowing way as they started. Be wary of those who are supremely friendly and "nice" through the whole conversation – it can be a huge cover up to protect their insecurities and their fear of losing status, etc, so be very gentle but also clear. Be sure to keep yourself in the space that there is nothing wrong with them, their data or how they are being. How they are responding is totally in line with who they are and their needs – it makes total sense. But at the same time, you can look for observations of your own.

Start looking for observations and data about their behaviour right at the very beginning – how they responded to initial invitations, emails, setting up the meeting, greeting you, introducing themselves, dealing with your needs or requests, managing their personal space, dealing with interruptions and, of course, how they respond to you all the way through your conversation. If you suspect you might be having to go to this stage (you usually have a sense early on), then start to take particular note of things that they do that do not work that well for you. Look out for examples of what the data is saying. Pay attention to how often they interrupt you, how well they answer your questions, how much attention and respect they show your ideas, note the specific words they use. In addition to noting what they do, notice how you feel and respond to these behaviours. Pay particular attention if you feel put down, unmotivated, ignored, put out, small, a lesser being, etc. Be sure you do not get hooked by these reactions but notice them before you put them to the side and get back to being a powerful coach.

You may need to make a physical note of specific words they use. You may want to simply jot down a tally of how many times they interrupt you. It is important not to forget what they are doing and saying and then to pick your moment to present this evidence in the most powerful way. Try to gather evidence of specific behaviours so that you can be really clear how many times they have done X or have not done Y. Look to find more than just one example. Two or three is much more powerful, as one example can be excused. Keep a note in case your level two fails.

Let's assume you are coaching at level two and it is not working that well. Several attempts and they are still justifying their poor data and excusing it. Look at the time – if you are approaching half time then now is the right moment to go to level three. You wait until the next bit of pertinent data and here is how it might go:

> **EXAMPLE**
>
> You calmly and clearly say, *"Here is some more data on your listening and respect of others. This is really interesting because I have noticed that you have interrupted me three times in the last 20 minutes. I've noticed that it has left me feeling more and more demotivated to speak up in this conversation – as it feels like you don't really want my input. That's OK of course but I'm not sure if this is what you really want from this session and this may be what is happening with your team... what do you think?"*

You need to leave lots of gaps through this conversation as they will hopefully be thinking hard about what you have just said. They are likely to be shocked. People will not usually give them this sort of direct feedback and it is unlikely they will be called to justify themselves when the other person is not upset with them. You are simply sharing your experience of them with the intention to support and empower them through this exploration. You need to take care not to leave them with a sense that they have done something wrong. Any reaction you may have to them has a positive and negative side and a set of consequences – make sure you clearly highlight what these might be. Make sure they know you are OK with them and you are still committed to them and their development, ie make sure they feel safe.

This is often all you need to say at this stage as this usually opens up a whole other level of exploration and coaching for them. However, the real tough ones will take the feedback on the chin (or pretend to) and hold on so you have to go to the next stage:

LEVEL FOUR: Acknowledge lack of openness, declare session over and part as friends!

You need to time this right as this final and rather drastic stage of managing resistance is always effective and can be quite dramatic. It is a brilliant last-resort position though, and once you have gained confidence with this you will forever know you can handle anyone.

You have worked very hard trying to encourage them to see what their data is really saying to them. Their resistance is very clear, they are not seeing anything much, they are not listening to your input and they are not answering your questions fully. You have tried all the good questions and asked lots about impact and you yourself have shared. Nothing. Key is making sure that you reach this stage about halfway through your session – too early feels a bit feeble and too late can be mistaken as simply an early finish. Once you have reached the magic timeslot for level four, this is what you say:

> ### EXAMPLE
>
> Again, you are calm and friendly and you start to pack up your notebook, etc, saying,
>
> *"Do you know, I am thinking this is a bit of a waste of time. You don't seem particularly interested in my input on your 360 degree feedback report so why don't we both use our time more productively and part on good terms..."* and keep packing up, smiling and genuinely feeling happy that you have terminated this tortuous session.
>
> The typical response to this is then, *"Oh no, of course not, let's get back to the report... please let's keep going"*, in which case you engage again and they are likely to now be open. Alternatively they may respond with a *"Yes, all right, bye then"* and you both go your separate ways.

As you can see both these scenarios give you back a level of control in this coaching, allow you to acknowledge that they are not being coachable, that it is OK not being coachable and giving them the option to turn around. You have to be happy with either result for this level of intervention to work, but in my experience, however it turns out it is totally fine for you. There may be consequences for them for curtailing the session (or there may not), but either way they are choosing this route and they are taking the consequences. This may be the transformational angle of their 360 degree feedback. In the very few cases of level four resistance I have experienced (three I reckon), two have decided to engage (finally) and one has walked. This one individual resigned soon after and everyone was relieved, so it may have served to hasten this process and their resistance to the 360 degree feedback may have been simply reflecting the current state of their commitment to the company. All good!

Key to this level is that once you know how it works and know you can do this, you can then be 100% confident you can handle any resistance. This allows you to relax and be present and be as powerful as you can be.

SUMMARY

Once you truly know that you are armed with this hierarchy of interventions you do not need to worry about your skill or your ability to get through or whether they will get value from their data. However your participant is, whether they are hiding their upset, refusing to see the tricky stuff or whether they are falsely reassured or just determined to be mildly unimpressed by the whole thing – however they are, you can be confident you can handle it and them. All you have to do is to follow the *Discovery* steps and apply the four levels of intervention and you will get a great result. You might even have fun in the process.

C H A P T E R   8

360 degree feedback data is easy to misinterpret

"All things are subject to interpretation; whichever interpretation prevails at a given time is a function of power and not truth."

Friedrich Nietzsche

Compared with psychometric profiles, 360 degree feedback data (in the UK anyhow) can appear very straightforward and easy to understand. In fact the reports are designed with that aim in mind – to be clear and easy for a non-trained reader to follow and reach reasonable conclusions. However, you do not want to be misled into thinking that this "ease of reading" means that the most useful and accurate interpretation will be made! And that is before you factor in the emotional responses that might be going on in the mind of the reader that will undoubtedly cloud the full detailed and objective processing of this important personal information.

Nevertheless, because of all the factors we have already discussed that help the participant get true value and transformation from their 360 degree feedback survey, you really want the participant to be in charge of their report. You might even want the participant to be self-sufficient in working it through and moving it from data to a development plan. You may want or require them to talk with their manager about their data in order to form and get agreement on this plan, so in fact you really want both these parties to interpret the 360 degree feedback data accurately and usefully. And that is the case even when you know that their views are different in some (or even many) areas... how on earth can we reasonably expect this to happen? If they do not interpret it accurately, both parties can come to conclusions that are at best confusing and at worst totally unfair.

The aspect of interpretation is, as you can see, quite difficult. You want to trust that everyone involved will understand it right and work it through responsibly but you know they might not. My experience of working 360 degree feedback data though indicates that in fact you can count on many aspects of a 360 report being misinterpreted. What you can do is to put in place training, briefing, feedback and coaching processes ostensibly to support the implementation of 360 degree feedback without anyone really noticing it is about interpretation as much as anything else. With maturity and experience the general ability to work with this data will increase and expand but in the meantime you in HR can take accountability and responsibility for the interpretation. If you consider this your job then you will be able to make sure you only implement 360 degree feedback with the right support at the right times. You will also be able to have the final say on the organisational conclusions that are reached via the data. You might consider this a big challenge and beyond your remit to manage, but try it on and see how it goes – you might find it helps you be sure that you manage your 360 degree feedback project with integrity. Why would you want to run 360s any other way?

So, accurate interpretation is important. Let's be sure that you are fully aware of the major pitfalls in this area which, if you are not wise to them, could well trip you and your fellow participants up, so you must be the master of interpretation yourself. You would not want your important ultrasound scan or MRI to be interpreted by a novice and neither would your participants.

Common interpretation pitfalls

1. Ratings can be interpreted by referring to the definitions

Well, yes and no! For instance, you may use a 1-5 rating scale defined from poor to excellent where 3 is defined as satisfactory, 4 as good. When you spot a 3 in a report you may then think it is logical to consider this as satisfactory. When you spot a 4 from someone else you may consider this is a good and therefore viewed as better than by the previous reviewer. These different viewpoints could indeed be what these reviewers were meaning to indicate and this could be an accurate interpretation of their opinions, but it could also be rather different. Chapter 3 covered the possible rating tendencies so, if you are comparing different people's use of the scale, then you cannot judge this with any degree of certainty. If reviewer A is a particularly harsh reviewer then reviewer A's 3 could well "mean" the same as reviewer B's 4. One person's use of satisfactory is another's good.

In addition to this factor you also need to build in the fact that, no matter how you define your rating scale, you will not have definitions that are understood in precisely the same way by everyone referring to this scale. You can spend a long time working out the best, most commonly understood scale but you will always have a range of interpretation among a group of people, especially when there is a wide range of seniority and different functions, etc. To resolve this issue you can look to use definitions that are used already, although beware of the consequences of using your performance appraisal rating scale as this may minimise misinterpretation but psychologically link the process to appraisals and reward and this may not be what you want.

So, what can you conclude with any degree of certainty? Well, you need to pour over the trends, the comparisons, your data over time and across groups to really answer this, and run some statistics to check anomalies, etc. Based on our experience, if you are using a standard 1-5 scale (as previously defined) and your instrument is working pretty well, you can only really be sure of the following:

Rating of 1 (poor) means the reviewer has either responded the wrong way round (do check if there is one reviewer standing out as an anomaly) OR they have a real issue with this behaviour.

Rating of 2 (fair) means the reviewer has something to say here too. They may be saying they have a real problem or they may be saying there is something very minor – you cannot tell with just this information.

Rating of 3 (satisfactory) means that the reviewer thinks this is OK, could have a problem with it, has no idea, is lukewarm, is generally reasonably impressed, good but not as good as some other areas, average, perfectly satisfactory or possibly even a total disappointment! You simply cannot discern which of these it is indicating without further data.

Rating of 4 (good) means that the reviewer thinks this is OK, may have little information, could be lukewarm, could be very impressed or just mildly impressed, is very happy with this area, is perfectly comfortable with this, thinks they are good or indeed they could think they are brilliant! You can be reasonably sure it is a positive view but you cannot be really clear on the particular shade of positive. It will only not be positive if the reviewer is determined to give very high ratings due to a particular rating strategy, fear, etc – but you need to bear this in mind and check with other data to be totally sure.

Rating of 5 (excellent) means that the reviewer thinks they are amazing, they are very good, they are excellent at this, they always do this, they do this all the time (even if this is not appropriate), they are awesome, they are the best at this in their group, they surprise them in this area, they cannot be any better, this is a real area of strength or even that they are totally over the top! As you can see, you can be pretty sure this is a positive opinion, but once again you need to check there are no fearful or strategic "all 5" ratings as this may well lead you to a totally different conclusion.

Rating of NA (not applicable, no evidence) means that the reviewer has no idea, can't understand the question, is not clear on the meaning of the question, has not seen this behaviour when they should have seen it, has no recent exposure to this person at all, feels unable to pass judgment as they feel compromised or that this behaviour is not relevant to this person at all. Key to this rating is that it is clearly saying they have no view to give – what you do not know is why.

So, from this you can see clearly that a rating might give you an indication of a flavour of opinion (or non-opinion) but nothing more specific. What you need is more data and to see the patterns, the related open-text comments and the full context. And this challenge of interpretation applies to every bit of data in your 360 degree feedback report...

2. Focusing on one piece of data

You can see from the issues of interpreting one rating that, of course, you cannot be sure what any one piece of data is truly saying. You need to see the whole picture to get some clarity over whether a particular data-point is indicating "good" or "don't know" for instance. But there is another big factor to take into account when looking at any one rating. That is the unreliability of any rating. Any one rating might be changed if the reviewer completes the survey at a different time. This is a well-documented phenomenon which has led the world of psychometrics to work to standards of reliability for their instruments. There is an acceptable level of reliability of 0.6/0.7 which implies that the best you can aim for is that 60–70% of the results will be the same the second time you complete it compared with the first time, ie it will be mostly the same. A quality 360 degree feedback survey will ideally be operating at this level too, but the key fact is that there is still quite a margin of error to take into account. If one reviewer gave a 4 this time, they may give a 3 or a 5 the next time. Why are reviewers so unreliable? Well, you may not fully understand why this is so but you need to know that they are.

You can see immediately that this issue diminishes the degree of certainty with which you can interpret 360 degree feedback data and also guides you to be cautious in making any conclusions from a single piece of data. In line with this, you are advised to consider the concept of a "rogue" rating when you interpret a 360 degree feedback report. If a particular rating stands out in a report and is not backed up or supported by any other ratings, pattern or open-text commentary, then you can suggest that it is rogue and leave it to the side until proven otherwise.

3. Low ratings mean something is wrong

It is easy to assume that a low rating means there is something wrong and that the individual really should work on this to improve it. But there are a number of reasons for low ratings. The obvious one is that, indeed, the reviewer considers this person very poor at this particular thing – but exactly how they are poor is not necessarily clear at all. An example question is *"Remains calm in the face of pressure"*. A 1 rating to this could indicate that they react emotionally and show their stress with tension. It could mean that they start to get a bit loud and aggressive in how they behave, or it could mean that they look really tense and anxious when the pressure is on or that they start to make mistakes, or alternatively it might mean that they have no idea what pressure is but they are always tense and stressed anyhow! One simple clear rating of a simple clear question can lead you to many different conclusions. Even if you knew which of these it was, you would not know what this reviewer is thinking they should do about it. Just being tense under pressure does not mean that the reviewer thinks they should be more relaxed. And one reviewer's opinion is not necessarily a dictat.

So, once again, you need to look at the other data to really work out what this might be saying to you. This is where good quality and well-honed open-text commentary can throw the light on so much. The data can lead you to the questions, the commentary can give you the answers.

4. Ratings measure how it really is

This goes back to the question of "truth" discussed in early chapters. The idea is that the ratings indicate something of reviewers' opinions, judgments or assessments on specific behaviours. You simply need to remember and keep remembering that that is all. It is so easy to interpret a 5 on *"Shows respect for others"* as meaning *"You are highly respectful of other people"*. The implication is that this is so but it is not definitive. What you can definitively say is that this means that this reviewer sees them as showing respect for others. Even if all the reviewers rate highly in this area it still implies that they currently see the participant in this way. Whether there is genuine respect or not is another matter.

The key is to detach the reality of what actually happens, how they actually behave and what they actually do or feel from the 360 degree feedback data. Always refer to the fact the 360 degree feedback data is saying it is others' view, perspective, angle, opinion, judgment, assessment, evaluation, thoughts, etc. Someone may easily show respect in the usual ways but be considered to be doing otherwise for a number of reasons. These reasons are the really interesting bit!

5. 360 degree feedback data is right even if other data says something different

You may think someone is a great manager until you see their overall low ratings – or of course you might conclude that there is something very wrong with your 360 degree feedback instrument! You are right, of course, to question the efficacy of your survey if the data consistently gives you different messages from the other data-sets you have. There could well be something wrong. Often the questions are unduly complex or unclear or the competency framework has some overlaps and lack of granularity within it which can lead to average ratings giving misleading information. At an individual level though the key thing that can occur to bring someone's ratings down is a critical incident and/or an integrity issue. If some "wrongdoing" has occurred that is considered unjust, unfair or simply unethical, this can impact all the ratings. If you have specific questions referring to these aspects then you will be able to check these areas to see if there are clues.

An individual's data is really representing the current quality of their relationships more than anything else. This is where you need to encourage everyone to take the broad view of the data rather than overinterpreting low ratings. For this reason it is important to always look at the patterns more than the numbers themselves and your job is to encourage others to do the same.

6. Just look at the strengths and the lowest rated areas

Most people look at 360 degree feedback data and assume that the highest rated questions must represent the individual's strengths and then also assume the lowest ratings are the weaknesses that need fixing[78]. These are some big assumptions! Unfortunately this is a little oversimplistic to apply to most 360 degree feedback surveys. Highest ratings tell a great story of what most reviewers are rating highest. This will indicate the key characteristics that are strongly coming across in their current role – their brand if you like. However, the fact they are high does not mean they are OK. You might be rated high on areas of *"Engages others in goals"*, *"Inspires a positive attitude to work"* and *"Dynamic and driven"*, but this energetic inspiration could actually be a bit of a problem for some people, depending on what others need from you. If they need support, structure and certainty this could really be the case, but if others benefit from the energy in a currently uninspiring situation then this could be fantastically useful. In fact every rating on every behaviour has a potential positive and a potential negative impact or meaning. Whether a behaviour is truly "good" or "bad" is really up to them to decide, depending on the particular circumstances and their intention. They may have low ratings in *"Can see both sides of an argument"* and *"Consults appropriately"* but if they are aiming to stir people up and enforce what they know is an unwelcome change, then these low ratings may be planned and expected. It may still serve to give them clues as to what they might do to make the journey easier - depending truly on what they want to achieve.

You need to be really clear that the lowest rated data may or may not be a problem as participants will naturally focus on these "negatives". This natural overemphasis needs replacing with questions and a challenging of these assumptions so that the participant can freely make up their own mind on the topic.

7. Form conclusions from competency-level averages

It is tempting to think that you can use the summary charts to interpret a 360 degree feedback report – in fact sometimes that is all you have[79].

This can look like it is painting a very clear picture of how good the data is overall and how it varies across the model – the weakest and the strongest competency. However, the validity of such interpretation is totally dependent on the quality and integrity of the 360 degree feedback instrument. It will lead you in a useful direction only if all the data directly relates to the heading provided and also if it forms a reasonably complete picture of what the heading title is suggesting is covered. Here is an example of a well-formed competency and another which is not so well covered – where you can see that an average will seriously mislead the reader into a false interpretation:

Example of a well-formed competency

Respect & Empathy
1. Shows respect for others
2. Shows care and empathy for others
3. Demonstrates effective listening
4. Notices how others are feeling
5. Is tolerant of others
6. Treats everyone fairly

Example of a broad competency

Inspiring & Developing People
1. Celebrates team success
2. Trusts others to do a good job
3. Provides inspirational leadership
4. Initiates action
5. Addresses unacceptable behaviour
6. Identifies future potential in every team member
7. Creates development opportunities for others
8. Supports others through transitions
9. Removes barriers to change
10. Gives others a clear sense of direction
11. Clearly communicates priorities

Averages at competency level also belie (deliberately) the fact that there may be a range of different opinions lying underneath the average. If there is a high degree of alignment then this factor will not interfere, but if there is just one outlier in a particular competency area then this can bring the average down and imply the competency is weak when it is seen as strong by everyone except for this one person with a different view.

The approach needed to combat these risks of misinterpretation is to check out what lies beneath the overview averages and not to dwell on or form any conclusions if there is any lack of clarity within the dimension or if there are differences of opinion. The overview is useful to start to give you the picture but it is not a place for firm conclusions.

8. Form conclusions from question-level data

You can always look at the question-level data at any time when you are working through a report as this is where the ultimate detail lies. This is where you can see the granularity of what people have said. You can see clearly where there are differences of opinion, or, if there are specific questions with particularly high or how ratings, you can also see open-text feedback referring directly to the specifics if you have this functionality available in your instrument.

Inspiring Leadership	Self	Mgr	Rpt	Peer	Senr
1. Inspires a positive attitude to work	4.0	4.0	4.2	4.7	4.5
2. Gives a clear sense of direction	3.0	5.0	3.6	4.3	5.0
3. Energises people to work towards goals	2.0	4.0	4.0	4.0	4.5
4. Has an inspiring vision for the future of the organisation	5.0	5.0	4.2	5.0	5.0
5. Engages others in the team goals	2.0	4.0	4.0	3.0	4.5
6. Excites people in their vision	4.0	4.0	4.0	4.7	5.0
7. Has a compelling vision for success	5.0	5.0	4.6	4.7	5.0
8. Demonstrates belief in the vision	5.0	5.0	4.8	4.7	5.0
Average	3.8	4.5	4.2	3.8	4.8

Comments: Q4 "Tries too hard to make this fit with other peoples' visions which aren't always compatible"
Q5 "A bit too tolerant of rebels who refuse to sign up"
Q7 "Stronger focus on what we are moving away from than what the future will be like"

The main danger with this type of visual, of course, is that you can focus unduly on one specific figure, and we already know this is unreliable. But there is another danger which is that you can easily find yourself comparing one piece of data with another and concluding that one is higher than another, eg if there is a peer group average of 3.5 and a manager has rated 4 on, say, how effective at influencing they are, then you might start to wonder why the peers are rating lower. But can you really say that it is lower? Yes and no. Clearly 3.5 is lower than 4, but if you take into account the lack of reliability you might conclude that a difference of 0.5 in this 5-point rating scale is within range of the potential margin for error. You cannot therefore conclude it is anything other than "about the same".

Looking at a different example, if the peers rated this question 2.8 and the boss 4.0 then you are heading into a realm of "difference". Whether this is a statistically significant difference will depend on your instrument, but you can take as a general guide that, with a reasonably effective survey, a difference of more than 1.0 is a real difference. This means a gap larger than 1.0 says that you can be reasonably confident that this may indicate a difference of opinion. If this were your conclusion then you might follow by questioning: How might their peers see this area differently? How are they influencing their boss more effectively? Where are they struggling to influence their peers?

However, whether it really does indicate a difference of opinion or not will require you to look at the trends for each of the reviewer categories. If a 2.8 for the peers is really very low, eg they hardly ever go lower and often rate 4.8, 4.9 and 5.0 at item level, then this is indicating a real strength of opinion regarding this behaviour. If, however, the boss rates very high generally with many 5s and just a few 4s (and virtually nothing lower), then a 4 from this boss is actually saying something less positive about this behaviour. Looking at the boss's ratings you can then conclude that this 4 is low for them. Your end conclusions are then very different – both the peers and the boss are giving low ratings for this in the context of generally high ratings. You would then compare with self-view and that of any other raters of course, but regardless of others you would want to explore and look to understand why this might be. You might ask how they are attempting to influence these people. How is it going? How much real buy-in are they getting? A very different line of questioning!

Another complication with item-level data is that you might look at question averages and assume all the reviewers in that category have opinions at that sort of level. That is the very purpose of the average, that it implies the feelings of the whole group. However, there is a big flaw with averages. In fact there are three different types of average and each has their own advantages and their own limitations when it comes to interpretation. 360 degree feedback surveys usually use the "mean" but you can of course use the "median" and "mode"[80]. With a mean the 2.8 from peers may arrive from one of the peers giving a rating of 2 and the other five peers rating a 3... Or it could be one peer rating a 1, 3 of them rating a 3 and the last peer rating a 4. The question as to whether all the peers are thinking the same is not clear unless you have access to the range of data under the mean. If it were the first range then your questioning might be, how have you been attempting to influence your peers? How has this been going? If instead it is the latter distribution, then you might ask how the peer group has been responding to their attempts to influence. How have they been responding? Has one got less on board than others?

Question Responses - Intellect

Grasping Complexities

	Self	Mgr	Rpt	Peer	Senr
1. Identifies the core of a problem	3.0	4.0	4.0	3.7	4.0
2. Draws accurate conclusions from the information available	3.0	4.0	4.0	3.7	4.0
3. Makes effective judgments	3.0	4.0	3.7	3.7	4.0
4. Asks probing questions to establish the facts	3.0	4.0	4.0	4.0	4.0
5. Quickly assimilates new information	3.0	5.0	4.0	4.0	4.5
6. Applies knowledge to solve practical issues	3.0	5.0	4.3	4.0	4.0
Average	**3.0**	**4.3**	**4.0**	**3.8**	**4.1**

Item-level data therefore needs great care in interpretation. There is usually a lot of rich detail that can be unpicked and explored usefully, but you need to be mindful of each of the reviewer type patterns and really need to know the range of ratings for each data point. At the same time you need to be cautious in making conclusions about whether the ratings are indicating different opinions. As a rule of thumb, if a conclusion is not really obvious and backed up by other data or open-text commentary then assume it may not be valid and look for other things.

9. Look at the averages for the different reviewer groups

Looking at a 360 degree feedback report via the differences of the reviewer groups can prove very interesting. Here is an example of what this might look like:

Example: Company-own sample report

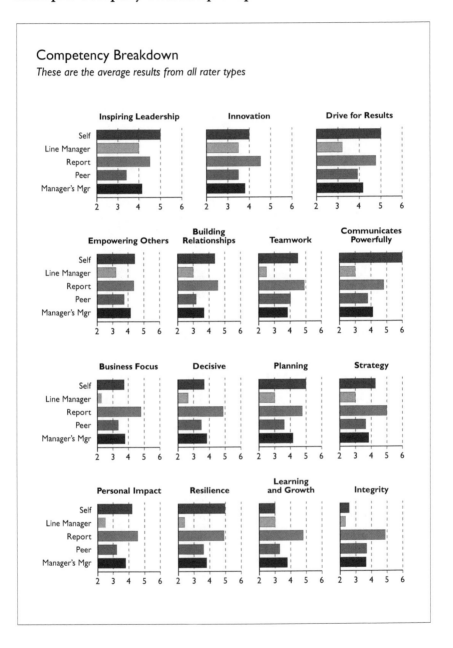

If your report is carefully designed you will see on one page how the different categories are working and what the patterns are. What you are looking for is the typical pattern. Is there one category of reviewer that gives higher ratings throughout? Which category is rating lowest? Where are the patterns similar? Where are they different?

The typical pattern may be that the boss is rating highest with the self-ratings high also on some competencies but not on others. The peers may show the same shape as the boss but be slightly less positive and the reports lowest with a different pattern as they are rating even lower than you might expect on those competencies connected with managing and motivating people. What might this tell you? Well it indicates that the boss may be very impressed or they might be a very positive rater generally – you cannot tell. Although you are probably safe to say that their relationship is a positive one. It might suggest that the reports have a different perspective and in fact that they are not finding this manager that inspiring. It is also suggesting that the boss (and the peers) do not see this. This might lead you to wonder if this individual is more skilled at managing upwards than down. Whether this is important to them is another matter...

This data is a critical piece to the complex jigsaw that is a 360 degree feedback report but it usually gives you that breadth of perspective, and generates a few general hypotheses which you then follow up and review by going into the rest of the data. This is an important angle but not one to dwell on or overinterpret in isolation.

10. Interpret a rating based on your understanding of the question

You and your participant can only guess what the reviewers were truly thinking when they were reading the questions and deciding on the rating. The best 360 degree feedback surveys include only questions that have been fully trialled in the particular organisation and level used as it is important that everyone rating the question has the same understanding (or as much as possible anyhow). The trick with this is to use language that is commonplace among all the reviewers, considering especially what is commonly spoken by the lowest level completing the survey. Wonderfully strategic and elegantly conceptual language may be used at board level but if the receptionists do not fully understand the wording then the data will be very difficult to understand and potentially deeply misleading. It is really hard for reviewers to say they do not understand a question when there is a presumption that they should, so this interpretation pitfall can be curiously invisible.

If you suspect reviewers may understand questions differently from others[81] then this question can lead you to ignore the data, but a more useful strategy may be to generate hypotheses, clarify assumptions you are making, and make sure to check with reviewers afterwards. Having a dialogue about the meaning of a question is actually quite an easy and effective way of discussing a 360 degree feedback data – it is not directly personal so it can be easier than otherwise for reviewers to speak up. In general though, if there is any doubt about the meaning of the question then further exploration is the next step rather than discounting the data or indeed making firm conclusions.

Even if you do not specifically suspect a misunderstanding of a question it may be apparent that this is actually always possible, with every single bit of data, every single rating. This possibility is indeed always there and should always be in your consciousness as a master interpreter. This quite rightly leads you again to be highly cautious in reaching firm conclusions on what the data is saying...

11. Presume all ratings should be high

This is a common and totally understandable presumption to make. Wouldn't you want all your data to be high? There is a problem with this idea and hope though. 360 degree feedback surveys that work are written deliberately to be a stretch for most participants. They are usually for the purposes of development anyhow, so you want the general flavour to be one that inspires and to be referring to a state that the best might be achieving just some of the time – an aspirational level. If it were full of descriptions of behaviour everyone was doing already then it would be less useful and quite tedious to read – reviewers would react with *"Well of course he/she does that, everyone does"*. This aspect of 360 degree feedback needs explaining though, as when you are faced with your data and it is looks like it can be higher, this is forgotten.

In addition to this there is another fundamental assumption that may lie beneath a competency model (and hence a 360 degree feedback survey) which is that it is truly the ideal that everyone is good at all these things. Even when many of these behaviours are antagonistic to others, eg if you are highly commercial, for instance, you are highly unlikely to be very empathic. Is it not possible? Well, there are a few who manage to tick all the boxes but they are usually operating above the level the model is designed for and they will still have strengths and weaker areas within the framework. In my experience these individuals are supremely respected and almost worshipped. These are the "irreplaceables", those few with "unique magnetic charisma" combined with a "brilliance" in their particular area. Their 360s will show this "hero" level of performance very clearly – there will be no doubt. The rest of us will look, for the moment anyhow, rather less stunning through the lens of a 360 degree feedback survey but it does not mean you are not doing very well and are seen very positively – expecting more could be described as delusional.

12. Presume the "manager" knows best when there is a difference of opinion

Most 360s show up differences of opinion so it is important to interpret these differences accurately. One of the "stones" to trip over is to assume that the boss's view is the one to take most seriously. This is exacerbated by the fact that the boss might also be inclined to take their own views as the "right" ones. And anyway, who would not want their boss to think they were good? The real significance of this relationship should be acknowledged and discussed in relation to the boss's 360 ratings. However, you and your participant do not want to assume that the boss's view is the most valid. The key question to ask is, ***"Who is the best judge of this area?"***

Some competencies are indeed seen as best judged by those senior to you, eg strategic thinking or managing politics. Some competencies are best judged by those you are managing. Examples of these include: motivates others, sets clear objectives, tackles performance issues, etc. Others are best judged by you yourself, such as managing performance even under pressure, being sensitive to feedback – not that other people's views are not valid of course, but you know better than others how you really feel.

13. Ignore the open-text comments as it is not objective, comparable or consistent

That is the whole idea of qualitative feedback! You will have a range of different angles and perspectives coming through and you can have comments that directly contradict each other. This does not mean you should discount them however. Each comment is valid, and if they are very different then this leads us to the question – *"What is it you are doing that has these two individuals thinking so differently about you?"* and at the same time you should definitely take care not to take one comment too seriously. The principle of triangulation of data still applies here.

Accurate interpretation of 360 degree feedback is critical in the responsible use of this powerful intervention – without this your participant can end up upset about something that is not really there or can think something is happening that may not be so. This can be very confusing, possibly destructive, and can seriously undermine the credibility of such projects – and as you can see it is not as straightforward as it may seem!

Here are six guiding principles in interpretation that may assist you. If you have identified some data you want to understand then:

- Check out how this data fits within the broader patterns

- Look for the links and connections within the whole report

- Generate hypotheses to explain the data and then look to check them out

- Before forming firm conclusions, ensure you have a triangulation of data, ie two other sources that confirm your hypothesis

- Drop your hypothesis as not proven unless it is glaringly so

- Consider that this conclusion is arising from the dynamic in the interface between the participant and their role/context/relationship

As a general theme, the key thing to avoid is overinterpretation. Let's imagine that you felt perfectly OK and you had your blood pressure taken in a routine check-up. If it reads high then your GP could start you on the appropriate medication. However, it could have been a false reading, it may not have been "that high", or there may have been a specific reason why your blood pressure was up at that time and there may not be an underlying condition at all – the instrument may be unreliable... The potential consequences of over-prescribing medication might however be fatal[82] [83].

SUMMARY

Most 360 degree feedback data is designed to be easily read and digested by untrained readers. The statistics are not that complicated, the figures not too tricky looking and the graphs are straightforward. This can lull you and all others involved into thinking it is easy to interpret. However, the 13 points described hopefully indicate how difficult this interpretation can be. If you were having an important part of your body investigated (let us say, your brain), then would you not want to be absolutely sure that the scans were going to be reviewed by someone who had, as a minimum at least, looked at other brain scans, if not by someone fully trained and expert at looking at such diagnostics?

CHAPTER 9

360 degree feedback can go horribly wrong

"The only real failure is the failure to try, and the measure of success is how we cope with disappointment."

Deborah Moggach

You are probably not doing a 360 degree feedback project in order to leave people scarred. You may have the best of intentions but emotional scarring can indeed be the outcome of a 360 project – at a number of levels. This chapter will look at the individual participant first, and then the broader team and organisational emotions and issues that might emerge.

> ### EXAMPLE
>
> I visited a very posh bra-fitters a few years ago and had the experience of being in a large plush changing room with a thick red velvet curtain on one side and full-length mirrors on the other three sides. I took a look and was horrified! Now this might horrify most people for a range of reasons but the sight I now had that caused my reaction was a clear view of the back of my head. I had not seen the back of my head ever as far as I could remember – not on a normal day anyhow (straight after a hair-cut being rather different). I simply had never seen it before and it looked different from what I had imagined – slightly different shape (more at the top) and more messy. Not so bad you might think but it was not as "nice" as I had thought it was my whole life. I had a strange, yucky sensation in the pit of my stomach – how could I have got this so wrong? I felt my head, I had a think and I realised it was actually fine. I had clearly gone about my whole life with this exact same back-of-head and things had been fine, nothing had gone horribly wrong, so probably it was going to be fine in the future too. Within a few minutes I had worked it through and was OK, though still reeling from the shock when the assistant handed me some garments to try on...

This is the process of seeing what has been in your blindspot, and 360 degree feedback gives many opportunities for stomach-wrenching realisations! Your job is not to prevent these but it is to prepare and support people through the process from first sight to full acceptance. In fact your job, working with the process of "managing resistance", is to make it easy for people to truly see these insights and feel the consequences – to help them get off the "river-bank of upset" and back into the river of transformation. So, given your plan is to have people see painful stuff, then it makes sense for you to be fully equipped to handle this when it happens and this is the topic of this chapter. If the process of working through upsets is not completed, people can be left with life-long scars and hurt. People can be angry, bitter, upset and humiliated for a very long time if they do not manage to move through this. So, this approach to 360 degree feedback suggests that you give feedback in the *360 Discovery Method* of feedback, moving through the conversation in the most useful order as described.

A parallel process to use is "managing resistance" which is a series of sequential steps and techniques, ie do this first, then if that does not work, do the second, etc. At the same time you need to look out for the 360 degree feedback "upsets" and deal with them, help the individual unpick them and coach them to a position of being "OK" with their data. I still do not care for the shape of the back of my head but I am not upset by it – it is OK.

The factor that underlies 360 degree feedback "upsets" is a sense that **something (or somebody) is wrong,** that things should be different. If you believe that something or somebody is "wrong" the way it is then you will inevitably feel unhappy about it. You will not like it. On the other hand, if you can be OK with things the way they are then you will feel at peace. Dropping this sense of "wrong" does not mean you do not care or that you have given up thinking things can be better, it simply means you are not giving energy to a negative opinion. Acceptance of things the way they are is the route to happiness[84] and satisfaction. Acceptance can lead you to see why things are the way they are. You might start to see the funny side of things. You can clearly see the consequences of how it is and can come to terms with this. You can start to see alternative strategies or you can be happy continuing exactly with how it is. You can see it as "perfect" – fine exactly as it is. This is a powerful and empowering position and can be your goal for your participants completing the 360 degree feedback survey.

First you need to manage the process so that upsets can be safely and privately supported, as, once participants feel upset and cross, etc, then they will struggle to hear people's views; they will hide and justify their position to maintain their dignity, and/or try to rationalise the upsetting data away. Human beings tend to want to avoid pain and this mechanism kicks in with this type of emotional pain. Your participants will not easily talk about it, share fully or be responsible with it – they are more likely to want to get the process over as quickly as possible with minimum disclosure.

This leads us to the question – how do you help your participants come to terms with their upsets? This is the upset-unpicking technique that covers most 360 degree feedback upsets:

1. Spot the upset

First you identify that there is an upset or negative emotion regarding the 360 degree feedback data. This might be really obvious – crying is a pretty clear sign for instance! However, most often, emotional control and professionalism kick in to have participants try to hide their emotions. Being upset at work is not really considered OK. So you have to look and listen and feel really carefully. This is your "deep listening" – listening beyond the words they are saying. Listen to how they are talking, listen to the subtlety in the wording they use, listen for the sense in their talking. Listen to how you are made to feel – tune in to your emotions. If you are "feeling" something then consider that it may be their feelings, not yours. Listen to their energy and pace. Listen to the rhythm – have they slowed? Look hard at their face and their posture – has something changed? Some tension, some sadness?

The first step is you being alert to the fact that there may be an upset (or negative emotion) – it might be anger, disappointment, irritation, hurt, mortification, humiliation, shame, guilt, deep loss, grief, etc.

2. Acknowledge the upset

Once you have spotted the potential upset then you need to decide what to do about it. If they are not being explicit then you need to step carefully as you may not have permission to discuss it at all. It is their upset after all. So a gentle acknowledgment of what you are noticing is an easy way to step into this arena, eg, *"You seem a little sad about that"* or even gentler: *"You don't like that do you?"* You can of course ask the open question, *"How do you feel about that?"* but this can land a little intrusively as there is a clear expectation on your part that they will answer and tell you how they feel and they may not want to do this. You can use your own emotions here to open the door to this conversation, *"I feel quite sad about that."*

Or even more carefully, you can leave space and ask them if they want to talk about it, making it really clear that they do not have to, eg, *"Do you want to talk about that or shall we move on?"* Make sure you give control to them. You do not want them opening up to you and later regretting it.

This step is a key part to the healing process as, if they open up and tell you how they feel, this will be a release in itself:

EXAMPLE

A young, ambitious guy in London was faced with rather damning data from almost everyone. He was professional but clearly mortified. He said nothing for a long while. He was tense, breathing deeply. He looked like he simply did not know what to say and eventually looked at me with an imploring sadness in his eyes. I gently asked him, *"How are you?"* He then fully expressed how he felt – he was indeed mortified and totally floored as to what he could do about this. The feelings were expressed and I asked him what his fears were regarding this data. *"I guess I am petrified that my career in this industry is over."* I could work with that...

---

3. Invite them to discuss the upset

If there are strong feelings and emotions then the cognitive brain[85] will not be working very well – they will be being led down quite a different path! Your job is to work out with them what the real route of the upset is about and you can only do this if they talk to you about it. It will not be clear to you and it may not be clear to them. All you can do is to get them talking but do not underestimate the healing nature of this "talking"[86][87]. You can ask about the specific trigger, eg, *"Exactly which bit of this page is upsetting you?"* and then try to pin it down, eg, *"Why do you mind your boss's view on this?"* You can try a general question: *"What have you made this data mean?"* or simply, *"What is wrong with this then?"*

Aim to clarify and summarise for them exactly what the core nub of the upset is. Check out which expectations have been unfulfilled by asking what they were expecting instead, eg, *"What did you expect your boss to rate you on this area?"* Check out if there is something they are now wanting to say or do, eg, *"So now you really want to challenge your boss on the fairness of their ratings?"*

You will know if you have got to the nub of the upset as they will start to relax, breathe and smile even though they may also be expressing their frustrations more at the same time. There will be more freedom and less tension.

4. Clarify the "should" and then the "make wrongs"

Underlying their upset will be at least one "should" or "make wrong", if not many. They might make wrong any of the following things:

The 360 degree feedback process	:	*"360 degree feedback is dangerous"* *"We shouldn't have done 360"*
HR for implementing the 360	:	*"HR shouldn't have made us do 360 degree feedback"*
Any or all of the reviewers	:	*"They are wrong"* *"They are making trouble"* *"They have no clue, none of them!"*
The 360 degree feedback instrument	:	*"This is badly designed"* *"These questions are unclear"*
The data processing	:	*"This is misleading"*
The 360 degree feedback process	:	*"We should have our reports in private"* *"We should have more support"*
Specific 360 degree feedback data	:	*"That rating should have been higher"* *"These ratings are just wrong"*
The company	:	*"This culture stinks"*
You the coach	:	(May not say this out loud!)

Beware that there may be a layer of "make wrong" overlying the real issue. For instance, the process can be blamed when really the upset is the level of the ratings and the opinions themselves. However, you need to deal with each one as it emerges.

Once you are clear what and who they are making wrong you can then go to the next step:

5. Clarify that the "shoulds" have been made up by them

This is the profound piece of the process. It is your job to point out very clearly that the expectation that lies beneath this "should" has been made up by them. You could ask, *"Why did you expect anything different?"* or you could suggest, *"So, you expected your boss to rate you higher than that?"* Check out why they expected things to be different... what grounds did they have? You can then clarify and confirm that it was quite reasonable for them to expect such things, eg, *"So, your boss didn't say anything other than positive comments in your recent appraisal?"* Clarifying that, given that fact or experience, it would be entirely reasonable to expect a particular result, and a specific reaction would indeed be entirely justified. However, the main point is to point out that they created this expectation themselves and to clarify that they did not really know, eg, *"You would think that a positive appraisal would imply your boss is happy with you."* You can then encourage them to explore why it may have turned out differently, *"Maybe they are generally satisfied and didn't think this specific area was that important."* It then becomes an exploration and you are in the realm of discovery again.

6. Invite them to drop the sense of "make wrong"

Just as you may choose to drop a pencil from your fingers or lay a bag on the ground or put something that has been messing up your kitchen top into the bin, you can encourage your participant to drop the idea that there is something wrong. They may already have done this, but if they have not you can ask them, *"Can you forgive them for doing that?"*, *"They are doing the best they can"*, or *"They are just being who they are, can you accept that?"* You might want to point out that they can still express their views about them and tell them what does and does not work for them. If they struggle at this stage, you may want to help them get clear exactly what they want to do or say, though at the same time you may want to guide them to consider their actions carefully and to take their time to process things.

Now you can go back to the data...

Some of the upsets are extremely challenging to unpick. One of these is when the 360 degree feedback is showing a stereotyping or personal branding issue. In some respects, of course, 360 degree feedback data always shows up stereotypes[88] or a halo effect[89], ie it shows how other people are making assumptions about an individual based on some, little or no evidence. If it seems that these judgments are individually derived then it is perhaps easier to come to terms with them as actions, and behaviours might be considered to be, in part anyhow, in their own control. However, if it seems that these judgments are derived from broader cultural stereotypes then it can feel that there is no choice about how these opinions are going to go, ie whatever the individual does or says, the opinions will be what they will be and have the impact that they have. This phenomenon is difficult to spot but in part there will be an element of cultural stereotyping in every 360 degree feedback survey. This is the world of unconscious bias[90]. Everyone faces a gender stereotyping for instance – whether you are male, female or in between! If you are an unorganised, highly commercial and very empathic woman then you are likely to see some rather strange data as these traits do not normally go together. And this phenomenon will be affecting the woman in reality – especially if she is in a highly male-oriented environment. A 360 degree feedback survey can lead you to discuss what you can do about this but it is a challenging debate for anyone to handle at a personal level.

What can you do about cultural stereotypes impacting you? Well, one trick is to speak openly of the oddness of the traits as this brings something hidden to light. Personally I have found that, as an experienced businesswoman working in a highly empathic field of HR, people do not take my business thoughts as seriously as I feel they should. This is particularly obvious when the other person is much younger and less experienced than I am and we are discussing a market I know well. When I notice this slightly lightweight opinion showing up I say, "*Well, of course, I am no business authority but I would say...*" It stops them in their tracks and they usually listen with more respect and a look of feeling a bit put off track. Putting up your own mirror to a stereotype can be highly effective.

Relationship breakdowns can be very tricky to deal with and they can show up in a 360 degree feedback process. A total breakdown in trust can become very apparent. This can be upsetting to come to terms with but the key thing to remember is that the 360 degree feedback is only throwing light on something that was already there. It can feel like something now needs to be done about it but there is no imperative to act differently. There is, however, a good opportunity to clear the air and recreate relationships from a different basis. This can take skilful mediation and support and may need a level of resilience beyond what is immediately present. These situations seem very difficult to resolve unless all parties are willing to tackle them and sometimes tough decisions need to be made to manage the situation. These can be very challenging in smaller organisations where there is much less privacy and no place to hide or move to or away from broken relationships, and you cannot move aside or change job or boss as you can in a larger one – which of course makes the stakes much higher throughout the process. As a result of this, full 360 degree feedback process in an organisation with fewer than 200 employees should be carried out with great care.

Some people can be very negative about others and can hold on to damning opinions with great determination and significant impact on themselves and others around them. Some cultures seem to allow these attitudes to prevail, others do not give them any space. Once again, they are very challenging to deal with. Open conversations and tough mediation and coaching can make a difference though. Supporting the individual in being OK with others' negative opinions is the usual strategy.

Nasty politics can become apparent and play out in a 360 degree feedback process. This requires management and mediation once again. In these instances 360 degree feedback acts as a catalyst to show the worst of what is really going on. This can be ugly to deal with and not to be considered by the fainthearted. If you suspect nasty politics at a certain level, you might want to take on dealing with this first before using 360 degree feedback. 360 degree feedback does not make the sorting of politics easier; it is that politics makes 360 harder!

All these upsets lead you to see 360 degree feedback as a catalyst for another level of honest, crucial conversations. A valid strategy is to ignore what it is showing up and get on with how things were (but with this new deeper view of what is happening), but you might suggest to participants that they can look at what else is possible, be in the enquiry and be curious about what is occurring. You can offer support in having new, crucial conversations and you can coach them to face the issues maturely and head on. You can also step in to support and facilitate the whole team. It is important that you yourself do not overpromise however, so unless you are clear and confident about your role in this support, do consider referring to someone with more experience. Team dynamics and political agendas are complex and as an outsider you can easily be the scapegoat for any pain that arises through these processes.

It is not just the individual's upset that you need to take care of. The organisation can have big expectations of the 360 degree feedback process and it can end up being a big disappointment. 360 degree feedback is not something that fixes performance issues, changes people or changes a culture, but it can be seen as such. If the 360 degree feedback is not fully managed and supported and integrated into broader developmental processes, then it may lead to individual insights but it may not make a dramatic and visible footprint on the organisation. There may be a range of views and perspectives to consider too. The CEO's view is just one perspective, and there are usually perspectives that you can bring to light on the 360 degree feedback itself that can help the organisation reach a clear and holistic view of what 360 degree feedback has provided. Doing a 360 degree feedback on a 360 project is enlightening and straightforward to achieve.

One potential source of disappointment is the aggregated data. When you look across a team of, say, 10, you may not see anything very interesting. The team members naturally complement each other so the averages will merge and the colour will not be obvious while protecting individual ratings. With a team of over 40 you can start to see more interesting patterns, however, and the data can show up broad cultural norms very clearly.

These are just a few of the more common areas of trickiness that need managing with 360 degree feedback. In order to minimise danger and risk there are key conditions that you can put in place and key actions you can take:

Avoiding disappointments: dos and don'ts of 360 degree feedback projects

Taking care not to overpromise will clearly avoid disappointment but this will not always manage it for you. It is important that upsets are spotted and acted upon at every level. This is much easier to do if you have designed a process that will automatically have upsets show up and where there is then space and privacy to deal with it. Accept that there will be upsets and only move forward with 360 degree feedback if you are comfortable with that. Despite this, however, there are some big-ticket ways of minimising the potential for people to get upset about 360 degree feedback:

1. Plan in debrief sessions and reviews at every level and with every individual – you can be creative about how this takes place as you can use surveys, focus groups, interviews, etc.

2. Be clear about what 360 degree feedback promises to deliver – ensure you have a full communication and briefing plan that is appropriate for all your key stakeholders. Consider your HR colleagues, the participants themselves, the reviewers below the participants, and the more senior group fully and differently. Talk about it revealing true opinions.

3. Be clear about the emotional journey that 360 degree feedback incites – run webinars, briefings and training and offer support.

4. Co-create the 360 degree feedback instrument and the process with key parties so that they own it and so that you get it just right for them.

5. Only move forward on 360 degree feedback if you are getting clear commitment from key parties.

6. Give as much control and decision-making as possible to those impacted by the 360 degree feedback – the participants and their managers.

7. Give the managers choice about participation as many times as you can.

8. Deliver 360 degree feedback as part of, and integrated into, a bigger scheme, programme or initiative.

9. When you spot upsets ask if they want help unpicking them.

10. Refer to "upsets" as opportunities for growth rather than problems.

11. Acknowledge and celebrate the new level of honesty emerging from the 360 degree feedback process.

The challenge lying throughout 360 degree feedback is that you want to expose new information and new insights. If you do not achieve this then the 360 degree feedback reports will be totally uninteresting and you will soon be rightfully questioning why you are wasting your time and energy on it. Alongside new data comes a "dark alley" of anticipation and a myriad of emotional possibilities – all of which is deeply uncomfortable and unpleasant. Even those totally committed to their development may experience this negatively. Your managers and your whole organisation will probably be tuned and trained to avoid and get over such reactions, so you, as custodian of the 360 degree feedback process, will need to be prepared to weather this storm.

Back to the dentist – you know there is often pain involved. The things that make the difference for you at the dentist are the speed and seeming proficiency of the dentist (and their team), their pain-relieving methods and bedside manner, as well as the service and feel of the treatment rooms. Applying these to 360 degree feedback, you are best putting your energy into picking the best tool and expertise you can find and making sure that it is delivered with empathy and care and an inspiring, larger context.

SUMMARY

The best 360 degree feedback provides real insight and new ways of looking at things, but alongside this new data comes the real risk that people will get upset. The other side of an upset, of course, is the world of transformation and learning, so you do want people to go there, to make the journey back from the emotional upset riverbank into the flowing exploration and experience of work. It takes real determination to unpick someone's upset, so have the courage and confidence to offer and support such participants and to use these techniques to challenge and prod at the unhelpful assumptions and conclusions they may have made. You can get them back if they are willing to let you.

CHAPTER 10

Find a partner for your cause

*"Coming together is the beginning.
Keeping together is progress.
Working together is success."*

Henry Ford

You want to implement 360 degree feedback and you know now how to do it well. You can manage that yourself for sure but, is that the best way of managing 360 degree feedback? And perhaps more importantly, will you really make the difference you want to make in the organisation this way? You are in HR to impact the people and the culture, to be a leader. Use 360 degree feedback as an excuse and a tool to progress the real conversations you want to have. This chapter shows you how to use 360 as a leadership tool.

Many, many words are written about leadership but not so many on how to be a leader from the position of HR. Getting committed to something is the key first step. Exactly what do you want to work for in the organisation? Is it the current vision? Is it an upgrade in the leadership cadre? Is it a culture that is healthy and innovative? Check it out. Make sure you are totally inspired by it, whatever it is, and then decide whether you are leading this or whether you are following. It is very difficult to be the primary lead on an initiative in HR but it is possible. Ideally though, you might want to find an inspiring leader in the business who is in a position of respected authority, eg CEO or COO, and look to see if you can be a primary follower for their cause. That is probably what HR was originally meant for – to help implement the vision of the leaders.

No significant cause can be achieved by one person alone. The bigger the cause, the more people need to be on side. So, as mentioned before, you need to find the "spine" of your cause[91], ie find the person who is as committed as you are to your mission – if this is the CEO then this will work well. If you can find no one then you are alone in this matter – and this is not a fruitful place. Best to adjust your sights or focus to find something aligned that does have someone committed. Otherwise you are fighting resistance all the way and that is not easy. Find your spine and you have the start of a team.

Let's say your cause is to develop your senior leaders. This may sound easy as of course everyone can usefully develop, but I wonder how open and hungry these individuals are? Are they coachable? What will happen if they do not develop? Nothing at stake? Well now, this sounds so unlikely one might start to think this is not even worth looking at... but before we decide this, let's look at what else you need to really make a difference in this area.

As briefly noted earlier, you need to have a vision of where you are going, what you would like it to look like. Bring it alive, translate it into a story. Imagine yourself going to work in, say, three years' time, and paint the detailed picture of how it might be. What does it look like? Who is saying what? What is on the walls? What are you being measured on? What does it feel like? How excited/happy are you? Feel those feelings – this will all help make this happen[92]. Write a whole page on how it will be in graphic detail and it will be processed by your brain as if it were true. Visioning your future is very powerful.

Now look at how you can communicate this vision to other people – translate it into a sentence or two. Test it out on others who are involved (practise before you get to the most important people) and see if they like it. Check out their reactions. You are aiming to inspire and motivate so work on it until you really know you have this reaction. You can tell when you have it as they will look and feel keen. Notice those who go for it and those who do not – this is critical learning for you.

Next, be sure you take a strong stand. How committed are you? What are you 100% committed to? You may be someone who does not generally do 100% commitment – fear of failure and a long-held practice of giving 70% to something and moving on if it does not come off can get in the way of your ability to lead. What does 100% commitment really look like in HR anyhow? You will know it when you have it. It feels scary yet fully satisfying (a bit like taking a leap off a cliff).

Be an authentic leader. Be you. Whatever your style is make good use of it. Find others to support you if you are not great at various pieces. Be honest with others around you, be vulnerable, share how it feels. Be self-expressed. Find a coach if this is not coming easily – this is tough stuff.

Be persistent and determined at the same time as flexible. You can hold the goal strong and be flexible about the "how". This is how you build the plan with others. Pay attention to where you feel like giving up, when you get upset or frustrated. Work them through and watch out you do not get stuck.

Lastly, you need to sell the idea to others to get their buy-in and commitment. There are four stages to this sales job:

1. **Vision** – you need others to see what is possible[93], to like it and know that it could come true. If your vision feels too far away from what is realistically possible to people then bring it nearer, take a smaller step. The more specific and vivid this picture can be painted the better.

2. **Opportunity** – you need to clarify for others what the specific opportunity is facing them right now – this is translating the possibility into a next step that others can see is a real opportunity.

3. **Action** – now translate this opportunity into a specific action that can be taken, whether this is by you or by someone else.

4. **Commitment** – ask for commitment to this action – something visible and tangible will be more powerful than words.

If you work with these principles, you will likely start to shift your focus from "implementing a 360 degree feedback project" to a definable outcome that inspires most critical people, eg, "Having a clear talent pipeline" or "Understanding our leadership bandwidth better", "Expanding our ability to bring new innovations to market", etc.

Every initiative HR takes on needs to be fully integrated within the organisation so you cannot do it alone. You need to have leadership outside HR and you need to have sufficient alignment within HR. You need great champions for your causes, so how can you spot the good ones? The best champions are well respected and credible across the organisation. A champion for 360 degree feedback has specific requirements – they need to have fantastically positive relations within and outside the organisation. They need to be totally up for development for themselves and for others. They are open to feedback and to coaching. They welcome it and they relish it. Ideally they have had painful feedback in the past and they can share their experience with a real honesty, showing a level of vulnerability and openness in doing so. They will be truly loyal and committed to the organisation and its purpose. They will be trusted by many and they will be willing to take a stand for a transformational initiative like 360 degree feedback. The other key thing they need to have is a real in-depth understanding of how 360 degree feedback really works and will be able to share their 360s with others so they can see how it can go – ideally sharing their actual data with others, but if not this, then sharing the story.

What if there is no one who fits this bill? Well it may be a tall order, so if no one ticks all the boxes at the moment then you might need to create them from a good starting point. Find the most respected talent developer and offer them a great 360 degree feedback experience – either for them or for their team. If you really have no champion for your 360 degree feedback project then you should be working on a different initiative first and it may be a timing issue. You are looking for the easy routes through your journey...

Not everyone will be with you on your journey so be prepared for the naysayers and the passive resistance. It may be within your own HR team and it may be in parts of your organisation. Use them as the source of critique, relish their resistance. If you are asking for their reluctant participation then approach it acknowledging their reluctance and ask them under what conditions they would be willing to do X or Y. Face the resistance but do not give up – as long as you still have the commitment of others of course. Work as a team member with your spine, you are not alone now. You will start to see your plans changing shape if you work this way. You are not in control of the process, this is teamwork!

There are some specific pits you can fall into with 360 degree feedback. Be careful "trialling" 360. You always want to build in pilots and reviews all the way through but you do not want to "trial" a 360 degree feedback survey as it will not be real enough for the process to work properly. Would you like to be asked to try out a dentist, go in with no pain, have the x-ray and exam and then be told you need some work done when you had no interest or money for such work? Whatever the result it would not fully test the process.

There is a range of different types of "partners" you can work with on your cause. As already stated, the most senior leaders are the obvious choices and these people are indeed very useful, although they are unlikely to have much time to give you. They might be great at the big picture and less useful at getting the detail right. For making sure there is sufficient budget they are of course critical. Be brave, get their commitment and ask for what you think is needed. They can always say "no" but a "no" is really only a "not yes yet". Clarify what their fears are, describe the risks and confirm what can be achieved with certainty. You may need to go slower but safer as there may be a hesitation to invest in the process as you really want it. You may want them to leave decisions like this to others such as a cross-company committee. Then it will not be you selling the idea, it will be them.

Your key senior 360 degree feedback champions might be your partners and could end up being your best sales people. Use them to advise you on how to progress, to find a mentor to support you. Use the project as a developmental experience and an opportunity to learn. Random leaders can be your partners as can anyone who really gets the potential value of 360 degree feedback and thinks others should be going through the process. Make sure you get them fully on board with how you really want the 360 degree feedback to go, as they could end up being loud voices making a stand for a roll-out that looks very different from your vision. You may want to look for opportunities to educate and share latest thinking with these key leaders. You can source useful webinars or workshops for them or bring in consultants to run briefing sessions positioned as consultation exercises.

Larger developmental or strategic change initiatives can be your partners. Look around for where current energy and resources are going and see if 360 degree feedback can be integrated into such programmes somehow. You can build the 360 degree feedback survey specially to cover the programme's model or priorities and everything ends up being joined up and in sync. This is likely to mean that HR or OD colleagues will be your partners. This can mean you have a useful ally but it may mean you have a political trickiness to deal with. Again, sharing an education and training in 360 degree feedback can be a good way of making sure the whole HR team is with you and happy to take your approach. At the very least it will bring to light where your views differ.

Other parts of your organisation can be your partners. Crossing organisational boundaries can often be very interesting and quite a challenge but 360 degree feedback can be a really straight forward way to bridge cultural gaps. You may want to take the lead with the project and be clear what is going to be "core" to all users of the instrument. At the same time there may be a number of significant pieces to the 360 degree feedback that you can give over to the different businesses/parts of the organisation. They might be able to choose their own front cover and email wording; they might want to add their own extra competencies to the core six; they may want to show a page in the report that maps the 360 degree feedback across to their values; or they may want to use the same technology but design their own instrument entirely.

HR colleagues outside the organisation can be your partners. You can team up with others in your industry to share ideas and even share a tool or benchmark. You can certainly ask for advice and input. Experts outside HR can also be your partners. Find someone who you feel you can trust and use them to assist you in selling and training in the 360 degree feedback. Business psychologists will likely be able to assist, as will OD consultants and some coaches and trainers. Business schools and local universities can also be useful to you as they might be venturing into some relevant research and be able to support and/or contribute to you and your managers.

360 degree feedback projects can be a bumpy experience for an inexperienced project manager. Challenges can emerge at every stage. The initial buy-in and engagement can be highly tricky. Senior leaders can think 360 degree feedback is a good idea without truly understanding what might be involved and where it might take them or their people. They might start to realise there are sensitivities and difficult information emerging from the process and start to have misgivings. Their commitment might then waver. One senior leader thinking 360 degree feedback is a good idea is not enough in any case – for it to truly work well you really need all the participants to be willing and eager. However, unless you have integrated 360 into the most awesome programme that is in big and urgent demand, you will rarely have every participant committed. All you can aim for is sufficient commitment from senior leaders and participants to allow you to move forward. Your job then is to sell the idea of 360 degree feedback to everyone "selected" as doing a 360.

Funding for 360 degree feedback can be an issue. It can be delivered at no cost. This is likely to be a process involving email, spreadsheet or Word documents with manual collating of data. You can create a macro spreadsheet to gather data more cleverly. Indeed, this was the technology my company used when first in business in 2000. 360 degree feedback reports are designed to be understood by the participants. It is their data and for them to understand, interpret and make conclusions. None of this takes resource or training. However, as you now know, there is a limit to the value anyone can get from 360 degree feedback without support and coaching[94] [95]. You can use internal coaches to give feedback of course. You can provide them with the additional training they might need to feel really comfortable and confident in working through a 360 degree feedback report with someone. External coaches provide something slightly different, and perform a critical function of maintaining privacy which is particularly important with the most senior people. You can ask for budget and make the business case in terms of £Xk investment to manage the risk of Y and Z. You can make a stand for implementing 360 degree feedback the best way you know, and if the budget is less than you need to put all your leaders through 360 then say you can deliver the process for fewer. Key is your commitment and being very clear what you can promise and the concerns you have. For instance, you might want to take a stand to only do 360 degree feedback if the participant has three follow-up coaching sessions as a minimum.

One of the challenges in 360 degree feedback is that you might understand the psychodynamic nature of the process and the need to maintain privacy, etc, but your senior leaders may not. You may find you are pulled to share data with the managers when you do not want to do this. If you are clear this will undermine your objectives then keep firm and refuse. You can always position yourself as happy to deliver 360 degree feedback "on the condition that..." Otherwise, if you are not happy to deliver it, suggest some other intervention instead (or first). It is your integrity at stake and this is worth protecting at all costs.

Exactly who is participating in 360 degree feedback is another hot topic. You may assume that the most senior person should be included along with those below them but this is a risky line to take unless the most senior individual is truly and honestly eager for this feedback. It is also debatable whether this is truly the best thinking. Unless you are the sole owner there is always someone above you. Even the CEO has a board and even the board has shareholders. It is also the case that 360 degree feedback should be designed especially for each layer/area of the organisation so a CEO should probably have a process designed solely for them with the input of the key board members. A top person going through 360 degree feedback that is not totally relevant or inspiring to them is not necessarily going to help your cause.

"Survey fatigue" needs managing too, although there seems to be a growing acceptance that there are online surveys all over the place now. The number, the pace, the timings, the reminders and the deadlines all need managing and the key is to be sure that your 360 degree feedback is standing out as one of those surveys that should really be completed rather than ignored. You have a number of factors to consider – how to time it avoiding holiday periods, how to pace it (in blocks or in one hit or on demand for instance), and how to ensure you maximise response rates. A key tip is to make sure there are real deadlines, as this way everyone will be working to a particular date and timeline. Anything non-real can slip all too easily. How many weeks do you give them to complete? How to monitor and manage their choice of reviewers? If you are clear there is commitment to the process then you will be able to work through these decisions and choices with your key stakeholders. There are many decisions you can give them to make – just make sure not to give them your "mission critical" ones.

A lack of trust will undermine your project. It will go smoothly if you are trusted as a project lead, if the 360 degree feedback system is trusted, if the survey is trusted as relevant and robust, if the coaches are trusted to be professional, skilful and confidential, if reviewers are trusted to provide honest constructive feedback, if participants are trusted to respond maturely and if the senior leaders are trusted to follow through on promises regarding sight of personal data. If any of these pieces are doubted you will want to rectify the situation and you may decide not to progress or to progress in a different format or context.

The 360 degree feedback process asks people to say what they do not normally say and people respond only if certain conditions are met. This is the – often unspoken – agreement. If you are not certain you can meet these conditions then you will be taking liberties with people and breaking your agreement. You do not have permission to "force" people to feed back that which they have previously chosen not to say. You can very easily overstep your permission in a 360 process – at your peril. People may really want changes to happen as a result of 360 degree feedback. They may be relying on it! Expecting individuals to change is a recipe for disaster however. An empowering approach to 360 degree feedback allows people to choose their attitude to their 360 degree feedback data, so you cannot force or guarantee how anyone responds. You help manage their upsets, etc, but you cannot make them OK or be sure they will change.

The main thing that might shift through a 360 degree feedback is that someone may see that their style is not appreciated by others and they may decide to give up trying to fix things and to get on with it or, indeed, to look for another job where there might be a better cultural fit, and where they might be more valued. If you can encourage people to focus on the purpose of 360 degree feedback as being to elicit and encourage more open dialogue and a better understanding of each other, then you are more likely to be successful in this. Nevertheless it will help you and the 360 degree feedback process if people share their data and have constructive, exploratory conversations about strengths, leadership style, behaviours, etc. If a 360 degree feedback is delivered without any other significant change process or coaching support, etc, then it may not deliver any visible changes at all. In fact, the more you are doing a 360 degree feedback in isolation and in order to "fix" your managers, the less likely you are to get transformation you can feel at an organisational level. Each participant may end up feeling more confident and reassured, with greater insight and self-awareness, but their new perspective and "x-ray" view of themselves does not necessarily shift the dynamic they find themselves in.

If, after the 360 "x-ray", the participant wants something to change then there is a chance things will be different but it is not guaranteed – more on that in the coming chapter. True transformation requires more than knowledge and insight. It requires new actions and a monitoring of reality.

If you give full privacy to participants, you may find that the very person who most "needs" 360 degree feedback is the one who avoids all support, does not share their data with anyone and claims to use their own personal coach to work it through. You and your more senior leaders will not know what is in that report and you will wonder what could have happened. People will be looking at what is going to change and will be waiting to have new conversations which may or may not arise. You cannot control what they do with this and how it goes, much as you might like to. Such situations still need performance management. 360 degree feedback does not take away the need to deal with behaviour issues. If anything it makes it clearer that behaviours matter and that people who are seen by many to be "behaving badly" need to be managed. There is nothing that substitutes true performance management unfortunately. Seeing how participants respond to the 360 degree feedback process can be very interesting though in these circumstances, as just the idea of a 360 degree feedback can bring up high levels of concern or resistance that underlie the deeper, more serious, issues.

> **EXAMPLE**
>
> A boss and subordinate in an HR consulting company in London were struggling to get on. They were "OK" after working together for over a year but it was still not great for others around them – as if they were pretending to work together. The idea of 360 degree feedback was proposed and there was a lot of commitment from everyone apart from these two individuals – one said they would only do 360 degree feedback if no one but them saw any of the results and the other refused altogether. A total breakdown was soon uncovered and both left the organisation within three months.

SUMMARY

If it is just you wanting to do 360 degree feedback then this is going to be very hard. You need to have commitment and partners within the organisation, or, alternatively, external experts outside who can help you gain buy-in within. For 360 degree feedback to be a transformational tool it needs to be a cultural match[96] for the organisation and fit as if it is the "norm"[97]. Being led primarily by HR alone does not usually fit this requirement. Your partners are part of the answer to having a smooth-running and effective project.

CHAPTER 11

Context and integration is the key to success

"We move from part to whole and back again, and in that dance of comprehension, in that amazing circle of understanding, we come alive to meaning, to value, and to vision."

Ken Wilber[98]

360 degree feedback data can be designed and delivered well as described in full in previous chapters but you may be disappointed to hear that this is not enough to guarantee transformation. *"Surely it is enough"* you say! Well, experience and data[99] tell us that it is not. Just try being subtly different in a well-established social dynamic, eg your family, and you will get a feel for why this might be. You are in a complex social situation and, quite simply, you, with all your habits and unconscious influences, are not even in full control of yourself, and you are certainly not in control of other people. But dramatic and wonderful changes can occur, so this chapter explores how the concepts of "context" and "integration" may be offering us some answers as to how you can guarantee transformation.

Context is defining

You show up differently in different contexts. You may feel the same but you cannot help it and you may or may not notice it, but you are contextual and your behaviour is contextual[100].

EXAMPLE

My family are church bellringers. Some years ago, my brother and I developed an online survey to look at what motivates ringers to learn in the first place and then to keep ringing. We launched it at a national roadshow and it generated great interest. Ringers were fascinated and we had lots of comments and discussion with people about the topic. Articles were written and conversations were had though it then got forgotten.

I was elected on to the Central Council of Church Bellringers three years ago. This illustrious body comprises about 200 ringers elected to represent all of the change bellringers in the world which might sound good but, to ordinary ringers, it has a bad image. The Council is known as bureaucratic, not doing much, very slow-moving, stuck in the past, a waste of time, etc, etc. I was on the Council in an attempt to change things and get action going to improve recruitment and training.

> This year I was running a stall at the roadshow under the label "Central Council". We were sharing the same (though updated) online profiler and people were similarly impressed although the stunning thing was that there seemed to be a layer of cynicism to get through before people would even try it. There was even anger about what we had done. And opinions about how poor it was before people had even seen the results. We were the same people launching the same profiler at the same event but at a different time and under a different label and we got a totally different reaction. It was remarkable. It meant that it was really hard work to promote this profiler in any useful way through this positioning. It was an extraordinary example of how stereotyping works and defines you and how I and my profiler were determined by the context.

Same person, same behaviour, different culture and you get a different result. If you have not experienced the real impact of shifting cultures (through changing jobs, industries, families or countries, for instance) then you may struggle to believe this. In every social group there are norms[101]. There are in-group behaviours, expectations and standards. These are difficult to spot if you are in the group as, by definition, they are the norm. Behaviours sitting outside the norm will, again by definition, not be the norm and the tendency will be to classify these as "not right". Those in the group may not realise they are doing this or why it feels this way, so it is very easy to bring a strong sense of "this way is right" and "the other way is wrong". You just have to travel across Europe to get an experience of different ways of doing things with each culture being clear that their way is the best way – why else would they do it that way otherwise?

My experience in the USA (as described earlier) gave me a taste of differences in norms. As my consciousness increased in terms of realising people were not responding as I expected, I realised I had no clue how to behave, ie I did not understand their "norm". I then started acutely listening and watching for what people were saying, doing and expecting. I started asking what the norm was. I was given information but I also met a response which said, *"Well, we do X and Y of course, why on earth do you need to ask?"*

EXAMPLE

I faced a cultural challenge when I was organising my daughter's ninth birthday party. We had only been in the USA a few weeks and invited her friends out for a pizza which seemed totally appropriate to us. People turned up and were very friendly but no one seemed to quite know what to do – should the parents stay or not? Presents? Drink? I was a bit befuddled by their reactions – it seemed obvious to me! After living there two years though, I could see how totally inappropriate and weird it had been. It was not the way they did things! My new American neighbours had been very polite and friendly of course and had forgiven the slightly strange and eccentric ways of this new English family. As a fresh newcomer to this culture I had been blind to the norms and had been unconscious of my blindness. The same behaviour in the UK would have had a very different result.

If behaviour is contextual then it then follows that 360, in providing data on perceptions of behaviour, is contextual too. A rating is a rating, it has no meaning in itself. If being very polite has one meaning in one country and a rather different meaning in another then you need to see the perceptions in this light. The idea of 360 degree feedback is to start to understand what the meaning is in the eyes of those who are important to you. Some behaviours really work well in some contexts and some really do not. If a behaviour works well then it will be rewarded, respected and valued. People will like it and appreciate it. But that behaviour will still have a downside to it. In a very commercial and driven environment a fast-paced, "bottom-line" focus will probably go down really well. However, the downside of this pace and focus may be that the individual might be heading for a burn-out situation and may be treading on others' sensibilities on the way.

If a behaviour does not work so well in a particular culture then people may feel they do not like it. It might appear as alien and odd and "not what we do". It might not be valued and it may meet true blocks and resistance. An individual, if they persist with significant non-norm behaviour, will likely be rejected by the group – physically, socially or emotionally. Being "counter-cultural" is not comfortable and it takes a strong character to maintain such a position with any ease. In our fast-paced, bottom-line-focused scenario above you may bring high empathy and support. This will probably provide something special to the group but it will not be comfortable for the individual. It may not feel valued or understood and may even feel like they cannot do it "right" – not fully right anyhow. The upside for you for being very empathic may be that you can get closely and positively related to others and can understand and manage the team dynamics. The downside for you might be that your empathy may prevent you from taking the tough business decisions you need to take – and even if it does not in reality prevent you from doing this, it may appear this way to others and then undermine respect for you and your authority.

360 degree feedback shows how you are seen to be behaving and it gives you an indication as to how well that is working for other people. But every rating for every behaviour has positives and downsides. Here is a list of just eight behaviours with both sides listed to illustrate this point:

Behaviour meaning	Low rating		High rating	
	'Good'	'Bad'	'Bad'	'Good'
Listening	Not put off	May not hear what others say	Super sensitive	People feel respected
Decisive	Time to consult	Can make mistakes	No room for others to decide	Gets stuff done
Strategic	Happy to respond in the moment	May not plan for the future	May not deal with 'today'	Sees the long term
Creative	Open to others' ideas	Likely to get stuck for ideas	May not have sufficient focus	Can easily generate new ideas
Sensitive	Not easily put off by other people	Likely to blunder into people's emotions	May struggle to maintain position in the face of reactions	Spots others' feelings and emotions
Supportive	Not expected to support other people	May struggle to generate team or help when needed	May sacrifice own needs for others' needs	People will appreciate their support

Behaviour meaning	Low rating		High rating	
	'Good'	**'Bad'**	**'Bad'**	**'Good'**
Commercial	Generosity likely to be appreciated	May make poor commercial judgements	May be seen as putting commercial objectives before people	Spots commercial opportunities
Organised	Knows how to flex with a changing environment	May leave things too late and not be fully prepared	May struggle to cope if plans change at last minute	Plans and organises fully in advance

If you follow this argument through then you conclude that every behavioural rating has a best job or culture or context that matches it perfectly. Most of us are not in that setting in some way, however, and there is no presumption that you should be either, but the benefit of understanding your 360 degree feedback data in this way is that it helps you "depersonalise" the 360 for the participants. If the participant can see that their data is showing them what lies at the interface between them as an individual, with their style, upbringing, experience, knowledge, motivation, values and needs, and their particular context, then they can relax.

You can help them let go that there is anything wrong with any of it. It all makes sense and is perfectly organised, being a logical result from them being in this particular context at this particular time.

Depersonalisation:
Focusing on the interface and not the person

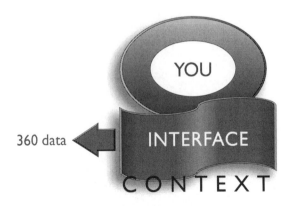

360 data ← INTERFACE

YOU

CONTEXT

And they are totally responsible. They have allowed themselves to be in this situation at this time (assuming work is a voluntary activity of course) so it is of their doing. They did it so they can undo it! Now your participant has real power and a sense of choice about how to move forward. They can accept this wholeheartedly and happily or they can start to manage either themselves or their context.

There are a number of ways to manage your context, all of which can lead to speedy and dramatic results:

- **Change your environment** – do the same work in a different part of the organisation, a different country, with a different team, at a different office.

- **Change your intention** – shift your focus, get clear what you really want, maybe drop an intention to, say, "prove yourself" so that you take up an intention you can easily deliver, eg, "enjoy myself", "support my team.

- **Let something go** – look at what is most causing you pain and consider dropping it. It could be a complaint or a concern or an opinion that someone is a certain way or that your work is going in a particular direction.

- **Look at new possibilities** – create new things you want that you can usefully focus on – it could be the longer-term picture, more choices, or alternative strategies. There are usually many different ways to reach the same goal – you may want to pick a different one.

- **Look for a new boss** – if you are not inspired by your current boss then get clear what sort of boss you really want and go look for one.

- **Change your view of what success looks like** – again, get really clear what you want and check that you are not simply focusing on what is the commonly considered view of success. Your true wants and needs might lead you to think success looks rather different and then open up some new options and possibilities.

- **Amend your own view of yourself** – maybe this new view is just fine.

- **Happily accept the stereotypic context you find yourself in** – let go that there is anything wrong with what is going in this area.

- **Adjust your career goal** – reconsider your goals and take one up that truly inspires you and that will fit with circumstances you find yourself in right now.

- **Play a different game** – if this "game" is not working well enough for you, find a different one you like even more.

As you can see from this list, even though it may feel like you have no control over your circumstances and even though your context defines you, you can take easy, bold steps to shift the current situation. All the steps above can be done in a moment – they are simple yet they are really tough steps to take if you are holding on and attached to how it is and to your own suffering. If you want to continue suffering of course, then you should continue just as you are...

This is the key transformational conversation that could make a huge difference to your participant. It is the conversation you can have at any point through the 360 degree feedback process – in setting up the project, on first review of the data, and after they have fully digested their report. However, the easiest place for this conversation is the 360 degree feedback session itself. The structure and techniques described in earlier chapters allow you to get to a point when you can make this point easily and will normally lead the participant to seeing things this way and to feeling relaxed and free to make some powerful choices about the best way forward. In essence the core conversation to have is this one:

Conversation to transform your context

Let us assume your participant has received and understood some data on how they are being perceived and they have some new insight. Then:

1.   **Clearly describe the current situation they are in** – be clear about what they do and say and to whom. Describe the consequences clearly – consequences for them, for others and for the organisation. Use the data you have and be graphic.

2. **Allow them to take in these consequences** – give them space to feel and process fully. Be sure that they have indeed taken this in – you will know when they have.

3. **Bring a sense that this is totally OK** – it is perfectly logical, nothing is wrong. Clarify how this is inevitable given their starting position, their experience, their style, their intentions, etc, faced with their circumstances and the particular relationships and culture they find themselves in. Be clear that this is like this because humanity works a certain way.

4. **Ask them what they would like to do about it** – give them space to think, to choose, to select a course of action. Allow them to think creatively and freely about what they really want. This is the space for possibilities.

5. **Suggest easy first steps** – you can mention that they might want to reconsider their goals, their intention, look at dropping an opinion, etc. Make the first small step really easy but profoundly transformational – perhaps a conversation with a boss, a partner or a mentor for instance.

These profound conversations are possible in 360 degree feedback projects, but, as has been seen, there are many aspects and emotions that can get in the way of such conversations. If you know you can deal with upsets and resistance along the way then this will give you confidence that the process will work out. However, the easiest way to bring in 360 degree feedback is when a positive initiative pulls it in – when an objective that is highly engaging and strategic begs for a powerful 360 to support and enhance it. It is the integration of 360 degree feedback into the broader conversations that really make it work. Integration means that potential sources of resistance disappear into the background or indeed, totally dissipate. But, much more importantly than this, proper integration means that the context will be changing alongside the process. It will not be left to the participant to decide to "change" their goals or job, etc, as some key aspects of their work will automatically be shifting anyhow. Or at least there will be an intention of a shift.

That intention alone will make a difference and make it easier for the participant to consider a new future that truly works for them for the next stage of their career. This is crucial and profound and remarkably simple to understand once you see behaviour as contextual. It is easy to consider that a participant could receive their 360 degree feedback data, process it fully, have ideas about doing things differently and go back to exactly the same job, boss, team, challenges, office, customers and objectives as they had before. Guess how easy it will be for anything new to happen and then how easy it will be to stick?

There are mechanisms and practices to support changes of course. You can take on new practices, get a supporting structure, measure and monitor to encourage your new actions, get a buddy or a coach. All of this is entirely possible, and with sufficient commitment and action, people can change whatever they wish. However, if the context is changing around them as well then things become so much easier for everyone. So, this leads to the question – how can you ensure the context is changeable for your 360 degree feedback participants? How can you enable the changes that are required to occur? Well, integration is one answer.

Integration can transform

Meshing your 360 degree feedback process into another process that is designed to develop and shift people means you are likely to automatically generate a new context. This very fact will make it easier for participants to move and be different. In fact, if this other process is inspiring then the whole transformation will likely become more inspiring too and this will help remove the potential resistance as well. A bit like – if instead of going to the dentist to check and then fix your teeth, you go on a whole programme of personal styling which guarantees you come back home in your new gorgeous outfit, with updated hair and, by the way, your smile will be improved too. I know which I would sign up for!

The important point here is to note that integration is critical for real impact. 360 degree feedback needs to be fully aligned and integrated into the language and processes of the organisation and the process is best positioned inside the biggest and most inspiring intention you can muster. This is the one you really know your top stakeholders are totally committed to and the one they are prepared to invest real resource in. It is business critical and crucial for future success. Work out what this is and, if 360 degree feedback usefully fits in this, then this will make the 360 easier to implement in all sorts of ways. Then you will be able to trust 360 degree feedback to deliver you real value. Trust me – make your objective bigger and your job will feel smaller.

The sort of initiatives you can look for are those that are seen as desirable by opinion leaders. Here are some options:

• A talent development programme	• Career development initiative
• Improving employee engagement	• Training needs evaluation
• Developing a feedback culture	• Culture change programme
• Identifying future leaders/VPs/ directors	• Enhancing creativity and innovation
• A high-potential programme	• Supporting the big vision
• Developing the leadership pipeline	• Directors' development
• Expanding the coaching skills	• Personal performance coaching
	• Performance improvement

Your 360 degree feedback will need to be adapted and designed especially for your initiative. Ideally the survey itself will speak directly to the relevant themes. It will be named and branded appropriately and, perhaps more crucially, the process will be tailored carefully to the initiative. The timing will dovetail and the support will automatically fall into the right space. There will be a broader positioning and briefing that covers 360. There will be a useful and timely follow-on. The 360 degree feedback data will be considered in the light of other conversations, coaching, training or data. It will be part of a bigger movement. Inside this larger and truly inspiring intention the 360 degree feedback will provide something very special. The 360 will give this technicolour, granular "scan" of perspectives. It will be a key diagnostic in a programme. It will be hugely interesting in this setting – not a thing to be managed and survived in itself. How much easier is that?

Integration makes the difference – it makes change realistic and possible. It makes the issues of upset and making the business case simply disappear[102]. If you want to introduce 360 degree feedback then look at the bigger picture first and identify where it might fit.

SUMMARY

Your job as HR is to be sure that your participants get the highest quality of coaching and support on their 360s. You can make sure participants are not left upset and scarred and that everything is done to have them reach the ultimate transformational conversation of, *"This is fine – what do you want to do about it?"*. 360 degree feedback is a powerful tool and needs to be treated with respect so you need to be responsible in handling and managing it.

360 degree feedback is best designed as a co-creation with your key stakeholders and in the light of the bigger and most inspiring strategic initiatives. You can work with others and consult fully and you can allow the content to emerge in their language. In the meantime you can hold the integrity of the process, the structure and robustness of the frameworks and the survey itself. You can fulfil a commitment to providing a valid, robust and meaningful instrument.

You can work to ensure all the parties involved in the 360 degree feedback are safe. They need full information, they need details on when, who, why and how. They need to know what is happening with their data. You can make sure no promises are broken and the integrity of the 360 survey is fully maintained.

You can be clear under what conditions you will deliver 360 degree feedback. You can make a stand for having the appropriate level of support, commitment and investment.

You can look to integrate 360 degree feedback into your best and most inspiring people themes and initiatives – this is where it belongs, as participants will not then be returning to the exact same context they were in pre-360.

If you are not in a position to fulfil all these then you can take a position that now is not the right time for 360 degree feedback and something else should be done first.

CONCLUDING REMARKS

If you are planning a 360 degree feedback project, you should now have a wealth of information to guide your thinking and heaps to consider. A key point to remember is that it helps to play big and it also helps to start small, and at the same time to be confident enough to co-create the process and the tool with your key audience. Let your participants take control while you maintain the integrity of the structures, and the core content and hold the intention. The more control they take, the more genuine value they will get. Be brave and let go – just like you might let your teenager have some freedom. Not trusting them to come home will probably mean they end up in your sight but it may also lead directly to their rebellion and upset as well as stopping them from learning and experiencing for themselves. You want employees to take full responsibility for their development, so giving them a strong sense of this with their 360 degree feedback is the trick.

REFERENCES (Endnotes)

1   360 degree feedback is the gathering of perspectives from all "around" the individual or the specific focus of the enquiry.

2   A change agent has a sense of will and a recognition that intention shapes and is shaped by unfolding outcomes plus a direction with a sense of purposeful exploration. An expert model of change agent makes clear use of data and offers expertise and value by conveying a bigger picture than employees have so far seen themselves. CRITCHLEY, B. (2001) *The Role of the Change Agent.* Found via www.billcritchleyconsulting.com.

3   CIPD WORK MAGAZINE (2014) Because business is about people. *Issue 1.*

4   CIPD (2014). *Megatrends: Are UK organisations getting better at managing their people?* Chartered Institute of Personnel and Development. [Online] Available at http://www.cipd.co.uk/binaries/megatrends_2014-uk-organisations-managing-people.pdf.

5   Carl Gustav Jung (1875-1961).

6   In physics, resistance refers to the ratio of the potential difference across an electrical component to the current passing through it. In other words, it is the hindrance to the flow of charge. LEWIN, K. (1951) *Field theory in social science: selected theoretical papers.*

7   GREENFIELD, S. (2014) *Mind Change: How Digital Technologies Are Leaving Their Mark on Our Brains*, Random House.

8   SCHÖN, D. A. (1983) *The Reflective Practitioner: How Professionals Think in Action*, Basic books.

9   PATTERSON, K. (2002) *Crucial Conversations: Tools for Talking When Stakes Are High*, Tata McGraw-Hill Education.

10 Transformation occurs when there is a change of position, an acceleration or deceleration or a change to the acceleration or deceleration or a change between levels, i.e. a "way out of a system"

WATZLAWICK, P, WEAKLAND, J and FISCH, R (1974) *Change: Principles of Problem Formation and Problem Resolution,* WW Norton & Co. New York.

11   A bomb turning from being an explosive to explosion, water changing to steam, tadpoles to frogs, cooking an egg, etc.

12   You are not in control but you can shape and create the contexts in which self-organisation can occur. Transformational change creates new contexts via new understanding and new actions, breaking the hold of current patterns for new ones. MORGAN, G. (2006, revised 2006) *Images of Organisation,.* Sage Publications Ltd. London.

13   MCARDLE, K. L. & REASON, P. (2008) Action research and organisation development, *Handbook of Organization Development,* 123-136.

14   REASON, P. & BRADBURY, H. (2001) *Handbook of Action Research: Participative Inquiry and Practice,* Sage.

15   A "champion" for 360 is of value. WARR, P. & AINSWORTH, E. (1999) 360 degree feedback – some recent research, *Selection and Development Review* Vol.15, No.3.

16   BRIGGS, K. C. (1976) *Myers-Briggs Type Indicator,* Consulting Psychologists Press Palo Alto, CA.

17   "Everything you've learned in school as 'obvious' becomes less and less obvious as you begin to study the universe. For example, there are no solids in the universe. There's not even a suggestion of a solid. There are no absolute continuums. There are no surfaces. There are no straight lines." R. Buckminster Fuller (1895-1983).

18   Magnetic Resonance Imaging (MRI) is an imaging method that produces detailed images of biological organs and shows structures of the body different from that created by other tests, such as x-rays or ultrasound.

19   In psychometrics, reliability refers to the overall consistency of a test or a measure. It is the extent a test produces similar results under consistent conditions.

20   Validity refers to the degree to which a concept or test is logical and measures what it is supposed to measure, and its results can be accurately applied and interpreted.

21   LAWSHE, C. H. (1975) A quantitative approach to content validity, *Personnel Psychology*, 28, 563-575.

22   KELLEY, T. L. (1927) *Interpretation of Educational Measurements*, New York: Macmillan.

23   Observer effect is also called Hawthorne effect. Individuals modify or improve aspects of their behaviour as a reaction to an awareness of being under observation HA, L. (1958) *Hawthorne Revisited*, Ithaca: Cornell.

24   Kahneman has identified fast and slow decisions. KAHNEMAN, D. (2011) *Thinking Fast and Slow*, Farrar, Strau and Giroux. New York.

25   BRIER, S. 2008. Bateson and Peirce on the pattern that connects and the sacred. *A Legacy for Living Systems*, Springer.

26   PATTERSON, K. & GRENNY, J. (2007) *Influencer: The Power To Change Anything*, Tata McGraw-Hill Education.

27   In Great Britain, one sixth of the total UK population or about 10 million adults smoke cigarettes. These figures have halved since 1974 ASH – ACTION ON SMOKING AND HEALTH. (2015), *Smoking statistics* [Online].

28   ROCK, D. (2009), Managing with the brain in mind. *Strategy + business*, 56, 1-11.

29   ROCK, D. (2008). SCARF: a brain-based model for collaborating with and influencing others, *NeuroLeadership Journal*, 1, 44-52.

30   Can be accessed online here: http://www.scarf360.com/about/SelfAssessment.shtml.

31   ODENT, M. (2004) *The Caesarean*, Free Association Books London.

32   The value of 360 degree feedback was first brought into focus as a result of a study conducted in the mid-1980s by the Centre for Creative Leaderships in North Carolina. Their study showed that feedback was desirable for an individual's personal and career development, learners were the most effective executives and that the organisations generally had a weak feedback culture. A decade later, the increased competition and renewed focus on the customer heightened the role of 360 degree feedback. LEPSINGER, R. & LUCIA, A. D. (2009) *The Art and Science of 360 Degree Feedback*, John Wiley & Sons.

33   In statistics, "regression towards (or to) the mean" is a phenomenon of averaging out. It occurs when a non-random sample of a population is selected, and two measures are imperfectly correlated. The average of the sample has the tendency to regress towards the mean. NESSELROADE, J. R., STIGLER, S. M. & BALTES, P. B. (1980) Regression toward the mean and the study of change, *Psychological Bulletin*, 88, 622.

34   The Johari Window was invented in 1955 by two American psychologists, Joseph Luft and Harrington Ingham, during their research on group dynamics in Los Angeles. It is an information processing tool for the purpose of self-awareness, personal and group development and strengthening relationships. The name Johari is a combination of the first names Joe and Harry. INGHAM, H. & LUFT, J. (1955). The Johari window a graphic model of interpersonal awareness. *Western training laboratory in group development.*

35   It is not expected that ratings from different sources will be the same. WARR, P. & AINSWORTH, E. (1999) 360 degree feedback – some recent research, *Selection and Development Review* Vol.15, No.3.

36   Recency effect is a phenomenon that refers to individuals' tendency to recall the most recent items on a list is higher than the other items. In free recall, the items at the end of the list are more likely to be recalled first.

37   A participant's personality attributes link with differences in over- or under-rating. WARR, P. & BOURNE, A. WARR, P. &

AINSWORTH, E. (1999) 360 degree feedback – some recent research, *Selection and Development Review* Vol.15, No.3.

38   Theory of social comparison was first introduced by Leon Festinger in 1954 and refers to how individuals acquire accurate self-evaluation of their opinions and abilities by comparing themselves with similar people. FESTINGER, L. (1954) A theory of social comparison processes, *Human relations,* 7, 117-140.

39   94% of all studies of self-reflection have identified activity in the medial prefrontal cortex. LIEBERMAN, M. (2010) Social cognitive neuroscience *Handbook of Social Psychology* 5th ed. John Wiley & Sons.

40   FESTINGER, L. (1957) *A Theory of Cognitive Dissonance,* Stanford University Press.

41   Objective is what has authentic presence in reality or that exists independent to the observer. Here, it is used in the sense of reality principle. FREUD, S. (1962) *The ego and the id,* WW Norton & Company; or logical positivism AYER, A. J. (1966) *Logical Positivism,* Simon and Schuster.

42   Subjective is what is effected by personal feelings and interpretations; some suggest that all our experiences are subjective. BABBIE, E. (2013) *The Basics of Social Research,* Cengage Learning.

43   Authentic leadership is a leadership style that encourages others to trust and follow the leader who has high integrity, a clear vision, promotes openness and improves individual and team performance. GEORGE, B. (2003) *Authentic Leadership: Rediscovering the Secrets to Creating Lasting Value,* John Wiley & Sons.

44   Available online at Talent Innovations: http://www. talentinnovations.com.

45   Outline of competency data gathering techniques can be found at Talent Innovations: http://www.talentinnovations.com.

46   An example of such processing was shown in a study demonstrating gender bias in academic selection: Moss-Racusina C., Dovidiob J.,

Brescollc V., Grahama M., Handelsmana J. (2012) *Science Faculty's Subtle Gender Biases Favor Male Students*, Proceedings of National Academy of Sciences, USA.

47   Dr Pete Jones is the author of implicitly ® which is the first commercial, reliable, online test to measure unconscious bias at work. These tests examine our biases that exist outside our conscious awareness and control. These are available online at https://www.implicitly.co.uk/ and http://www.hogrefe.co.uk/implicitly.html.

48   A brand refers to the image of a specific type of product, company or person and is distinguished from others. Characteristics are inferred and associated with the name, product or look. MALONE, C. & FISKE, S. T. (2013) *The Human Brand: How We Relate to People, Products, and Companies*, John Wiley & Sons. Wilson and Blumenthal.

49   "Whether we realize it or not, we are all brands. We all have qualities that shape and influence how the people in our lives see us, and how we see ourselves." WILSON, J. S. & BLUMENTHAL, I. (2008) *Managing Brand You: 7 Steps to Creating Your Most Successful Self*, AMACOM Div American Mgmt Assn.

50   LADKIN, R. 2006. Inquiry and Reflective Practice. *In:* CRITCHLEY, B., KING, K. & HIGGINS, J. (eds.) *Organisational Consulting – A Relational Perspective: Theories and Stories from the Field (Management, Policy & Education)*, London, Middlesex: University Press.

51   Buckminster Fuller refers to the strength of the most robust structure in nature – the tetrahedron, a four-pointed shape, which starts with formation of the first side – you and another. BUCKMINSTER FULLER, R. (1992) *Cosmography*, Macmillan Publishing Co. New York.

52   See *"How to create and maintain an effective competency framework"*, available via www.talentinnovations.com.

53 Individuals can hold seven (+/-two) items in working memory, MILLER, G. A. (1956) *The Magical Number Seven, Plus or Minus Two: Some Limits on Our Capacity for Processing Information*, Psychological review, 63, 81. Since then, this simple model has been replaced by the concept of a more complex working memory but the idea of the limitation of attentional short-term memory seems still to hold true.

54 See samples via the Talent Innovations website or a demo: http://www.talentinnovations.com.

55 See practical guide to techniques for designing competency frameworks in paper *How to create and maintain an effective competency framework*, available via http://www.talentinnovations.com.

56 See the blog written on rating scales at Talent Innovations: http://www.talentinnovations.com.

57 The value of a pilot group, WARR, P. & AINSWORTH, E. (1999) 360 degree feedback – some recent research, *Selection and Development Review* Vol.15, No.3.

58 The limbic area of the brain, ROCK, D., DIXON, P. & OCHSNER, K. (2010) 'Turn the 360 around: why feedback doesn't work and how to do it better', *NeuroLeadership Journal*, 3, 78-86.

59 The pre-frontal cortex (PFC) of the brain, ROCK, D., DIXON, P. & OCHSNER, K. (2010) 'Turn the 360 around: why feedback doesn't work and how to do it better', *NeuroLeadership Journal*, 3, 78-86.

60 Success is seen as dependent on whether we approach our goals with a fixed or a growth mindset. A growth mindset is defined as being a "learn-and-help-learn" framework. DWECK, CS. (2012) *Mindset: How You Can Fulfil Your Potential*, Robinson.

61 According to David Rock, an individual's ability to learn is influenced by the level of neurotransmitters. Learning can be increased by increasing the ability to focus, such as using humour. However, it is easier to increase brain chemicals triggered by a threat response which can hamper the learning response. Therefore, threat

responses during learning should be focused, ROCK, D., DIXON, P. & OCHSNER, K. (2010) 'Turn the 360 around: why feedback doesn't work and how to do it better', *NeuroLeadership Journal*, 3, 78-86.

62   ROCK, D. (2009) Managing with the brain in mind. *Strategy + business*, 56, 1-11.

63   ADLER, A (1870-1937) may have been the first to refer to the assumption that human beings are creative meaning makers.

64   See blog describing the depersonalisation technique at Talent Innovations: http://www.talentinnovations.com.

65   Examples of materials used to brief 360 can be accessed via Talent Innovations: http://www.talentinnovations.co.uk.

66   Employers and Workmen Act 1875 which gave workers some rights.

67   Workers welfare was championed by the Rowntree movement in the early part of the 20th century with "personnel management" (as HR was formerly known) emerging after the second world war.

68   Institute of Employment Studies (IES) (1990) *From People to Profits, the HR link to the service-profit chain.*

69   WELCH, H. G., SCHWARTZ, L. & WOLOSHIN, S. (2011) *Overdiagnosed: Making People Sick in the Pursuit of Health*, Beacon Press.

70   KUHN, T. S. (2012) *The Structure of Scientific Revolutions*, University of Chicago Press.

71   The process of hypothesis generation is an uninterrupted, unbiased flow of awareness together with a translation of the data leading to the formation of a workable hypothesis. NEVIS, E.C. (1987) *Organisational Consulting: A Gestalt Approach*, Analytic Press, New Jersey.

72   LINDAHL, K. (2001) *The Sacred Art of Listening: Forty Reflections for Cultivating a Spiritual Practice*, SkyLight Paths Publishing.

73   EIKENBERRY, K. (2011) *Remarkable Leadership: Unleashing Your Leadership Potential One Skill at a Time,* John Wiley & Sons.

74   WATZLAWICK, P., WEAKLAND, J. H. & FISCH, R. (1974) *Change: Principles of Problem Formation and Problem Resolution,* WW Norton.

75   MCLEAN, A. & POWER, K. 2006. Advocating some theory – framing Bateson. *In:* CRITCHLEY, B., HIGGINS, J. & KING, K. (eds.) *Organisational Consulting – A Relational Perspective: Theories and Stories From the Field,* London, Middlesex University Press.

76   One approach is to review the "layers" presented – one of the methodologies described by Ian Watson: WATSON, I. (1991) *A Guide to the Methodologies of Homeopathy,* Miller Turner Printers Ltd, Cumbria.

77   There are "powerful questions instead of powerful answers" and "what leads to real change is not action plans, but some combination of courage and freewill on the part of the client", BLOCK, P. (1999) *Flawless Consulting: A Guide to Getting Your Expertise Used,* Jossey-Bass, San Francisco.

78   Not all feedback information should be acted on, WARR, P. & AINSWORTH, E. (1999) 360 degree feedback – some recent research, *Selection and Development Review* Vol.15, No.3.

79   Refer to *Inspiring Executive* seen at http://www.talentinnovations.com.

80   Arithmetic mean is the sum of a set of numeric values divided by the number of terms in that set. Median is the middle value of a set when the numeric values have been sorted. And, Mode is the most frequently occurring value in a set of numeric values. MADSEN, B. (2011) *Statistics for Non-statisticians,* Springer Science & Business Media.

81   LANGACKER, R. W. (1999) *Grammar and Conceptualization,* Walter de Gruyter.

82   WELCH, H. G., SCHWARTZ, L. & WOLOSHIN, S. (2011) *Overdiagnosed: Making People Sick in the Pursuit of Health*, Beacon Press.

83   GOLDACRE, B. (2012) *Bad Pharma: How Drug Companies Mislead Doctors and Harm Patients*, HarperCollins, London.

84   SELIGMAN, M. E. (2004) *Authentic Happiness: Using the New Positive Psychology to Realize Your Potential for Lasting Fulfillment*, Simon and Schuster.

85   "Links between perceived threat and reduced cognition have a deep relevance to coaching". Naming the emotions can assist in managing and normalising someone as this calms the amygdala. This then allows for more activity in the problem solving centres. ROCK, D. & PAGE L. J. (2009) *Coaching with the Brain in Mind.* John Wiley & Sons, New Jersey, Pg 364-635.

86   Naming the emotions with simple language lowers the arousal experienced and allows for more effective processing. LIEBERMAN M., EISENBERGER N., CROCKETT M., TOM S., PFEIFER J. & WAY B. (2007) *Putting Feelings into Words: Affect Labelling Disrupts Amygdala Activity In Response to Affective Stimuli*, Psychological Science 18.

87   Attitudes to 360 changed when participants had the opportunity to express their opinions and interpretations, WARR, P. & AINSWORTH, E. (1999) 360 degree feedback – some recent research, *Selection and Development Review* Vol.15, No.3.

88   BRETZ, R. D., MILKOVICH, G. T. & READ, W. (1992) The current state of performance appraisal research and practice: Concerns, directions, and implications, *Journal of management*, 18, 321-352.

89   BALZER, W. K. & SULSKY, L. M. (1992) Halo and performance appraisal research: A critical examination, *Journal of Applied Psychology*, 77, 975.

90   See Equality Challenge Unit review of literature on Unconscious bias undertaken with the help of Dr Peter Jones (a Chartered

Psychologist and Chartered Scientist with specialisation in unconscious bias) and Tinu Cornish. The report is available online at http://www.ecu.ac.uk/publications/unconscious-bias-in-higher-education/.

91   Buckminster Fuller refers to the geometric shape tetrahedron (four-pointed) as the most robust shape which implies that a team of four has a unique strength for team working – this starts with you "teaming" with another as your spine for a cause. BUCKMINSTER FULLER, R. (1992) *Cosmography*, Macmillan Publishing Co, New York.

92   BYRNE, R. (2006) *The Secret*, Simon and Schuster.

93   ZANDER, R. S. & ZANDER, B. (2000) *The Art of Possibility*, Harvard Business Press.

94   Follow up is everything. NOWACK, K. (2009) *Leveraging 360-Feedback to Facilitate Successful Behavioral Change*, Consulting Psychology: Practice and Research, 61, 280-297.

95   Those giving 360 feedback should be fully trained as described by Prof Christine Farrell, Kate Oliver and Andrew Geake. BAIN, N. & MABEY, W. (2009) *The People Advantage: Improving Results Through Better Selection and Performance.* Macmillan Press, Basingstoke, England.

96   A study by GEAKE, FARRELL & OLIVER (1998) identified that the sense that a 360 process is culturally inappropriate is a potential source of resistance. WARR, P. & AINSWORTH, E. (1999) 360 degree feedback – some recent research, *Selection and Development Review* Vol.15, No.3.

97   Actions within the current organisational norms are a critical part to a behavioural change intervention. FISHBEIN, M. & AJZEN, I. (2010), *Predicting and Changing Behavior: The Reasoned Action Approach*, Psychology Press, New York.

98   Ken Wilber has authored over 25 books, is the founder of the thinktank Integral Institute and is one of the most influential philosophers of the 21st century. His influential book *A Theory of Everything* helps to

enrich all disciplines through an understanding of how and where everyone fits in relation to all the others, and by doing so, reveals the possibilities of a more sustainable future for all of us.

99   STACEY, R. D. (1996) *Complexity and Creativity in Organizations*, Berrett-Koehler Publishers.

100   According to the contingent view of leadership, that leadership changes according to, among other things, the rate of change in the organisation, MANNING, T. (2013) *A "contingent" view of leadership: 360 degree assessments of leadership behaviours in different contexts*, Industrial and Commercial Training, 45, 343-351.

101   HOFSTEDE, G. (1983) National cultures in four dimensions: A research-based theory of cultural differences among nations, *International Studies of Management & Organization*, 46-74.

102   WILBER, K. (2001) *A Theory of Everything: An Integral Vision for Business, Politics, Science, and Spirituality*, Shambhala Publications.

ABOUT THE AUTHOR

Elva Ainsworth was born into a family of people watchers and has cultivated a real love of people-pattern spotting. This combination led her to a career in HR after a psychology degree at Bristol University. In HR she enjoyed implementing the brand new psychometrics as well as designing culture change and personal development tools. In 1994 she focused on her love of psychometrics by joining SHL (now CEB), the leading business psychologists, where she managed the 360 degree feedback and management development practice in both the UK and the USA.

Qualifying in homeopathy was combined with her OD perspective to feed a strong appetite for a new approach to giving feedback. Having experienced therapeutic processes that enabled easy paradigm shifts, Elva was sure there was a new way. She looked to guarantee "light-bulb" moments while supporting people through and out of the emotional upsets that often arise from 360 degree feedback. She was on a mission! Her hypothesis was that "personalisation" of 360 degree feedback surveys would make a difference by encouraging ownership of the development process and also that privacy would give sufficient safety for real learning to occur. The result of her application and experience is this book.